INTO THE OPEN

We gratefully acknowledge the support of the Canada Council for the Arts and the Ontario Arts Council for our publishing program. We also acknowledge the financial support of the Government of Canada.

Cover artwork: Frederick Horsman Varley, "View from the Artist's Bedroom, Jericho Beach, 1929," oil on canvas, 99.4 x 83.8 cm. Collection of the Winnipeg Art Gallery. Acquired with the assistance of the Women's Committee and the Woods-Harris Trust Fund No. 1, G-72-7. Photo: Ernest Mayer. Used with permission.

Library and Archives Canada Cataloguing in Publication

McCaslin, Susan, 1947-
[Poems. Selections]
        Into the open : poems new and selected / Susan McCaslin.
(Inanna poetry & fiction series)
Issued in print and electronic formats.
ISBN 978-1-77133-465-5 (softcover). -- ISBN 978-1-77133-466-2 (epub). --
ISBN 978-1-77133-467-9 (Kindle). -- ISBN 978-1-77133-468-6 (pdf)

        I. Title. II. Series: Inanna poetry and fiction series

PS8575.C43A6 2017   C813'.54   C2017-905431-7
                                                           C2017-905432-5

Printed and bound in Canada

Inanna Publications and Education Inc.
210 Founders College, York University
4700 Keele Street, Toronto, Ontario, Canada M3J 1P3
Telephone: (416) 736-5356 Fax: (416) 736-5765
Email: inanna.publications@inanna.ca
Website: www.inanna.ca

MIX
Paper from
responsible sources
FSC
www.fsc.org   FSC® C004071

INTO THE OPEN
Poems New and Selected

Susan McCaslin

inanna poetry & fiction series

INANNA Publications and Education Inc.
Toronto, Canada

For my beloved Mark

Contents

from *Flying Wounded* (2000)

from *A Plot of Light* (2004)

from *The Disarmed Heart* (2014)

Appendix: Selections from Early Chapbooks

With all its eyes the natural world looks out
into the open.

—Rainer Maria Rilke, "Eighth Duino Elegy,"
(trans. Stephen Mitchell)

Foreword

Selecting from Susan McCaslin's eighteen-book oeuvre *Into the Open: Poems New and Selected* has been a pilgrimage through her poetic and spiritual evolution. Her visionary poetscapes conjure William Blake, Thomas Merton, Greco-Roman mythology, angels, the Canadian mystic Olga Park, John of Patmos, Teresa of Avila, Henry Vaughan, Lao Tzu, Han Shan, Mary Magdalene, and other unitive mystics of many cultures, faiths, and eras. Such diversity suggests the range and reach of McCaslin's work. Here is a poet at the peak of her powers.

McCaslin's initial exploration into the mystical streams of Christianity continually extend *into the open*. The movement of her body of work to an inclusive, synergistic mode of seeing and being enacts a steady growth toward the need for kindness and empathy. Her poetic viewpoint broadens to absorb the good in the world and the longing to act for justice.

Richly varied and linked themes showcase McCaslin's innovative craft in both free verse and classical forms like the sonnet sequence, ode, heroic sestet, glosa, villanelle, palindrome, triolet, and pantoum. McCaslin's poems invite the reader to care for all sentience, to open to wonder and gratitude, and to enter an ekphrastic enquiry into Paul Cézanne's artistic experience. In the process she explores the divine feminine, ecology and social justice, imagination's transformative power, *ars poetica*, the mysteries of the creative process, and our stewardship of the earth.

McCaslin's intuitive sense of metaphor is evident in her chapbook and book titles: *Motions of the Hearts* (1978); *Kindling* (1979); *The Seven Sleepers* (1979); *Conversing with Paradise* (1986); *Locutions* (1995); *Veil/ Unveil* (1997); *Light Housekeeping* (1997); *Into the Open* (1999); *The*

Altering Eye (2000); *Flying Wounded* (2000); *Common Longing* (2001); *At the Mercy Seat* (2003); *A Plot of Light* (2004); *Lifting the Stone* (2007); *Demeter Goes Skydiving* (2011); *The Disarmed Heart* (2014); *Painter, Poet, Mountain: After Cézanne* (2016), and her previously unpublished book *Lineage*. The resonant titles embody her approach to poetry, faith and life itself: light-heartedness combined with an exuberant twinkle and a compassionate eye. These poems play, grieve, and love their way throughout the plant and animal cornucopia.

Few poets nod to the numinous nowadays, but Susan McCaslin redeems that lapse. Choosing and omitting poems from this plethora of work was a delicious and difficult challenge. I selected for thematic relevance and striking metaphors that carry the visionary imprint of McCaslin's altering eye. Immersion in her poetics is to stretch star-ward (star-word) into the open realm of gratitude and grace that comes to the receptive and *disarmed heart*.

—Katerina Vaughan Fretwell

On the Poetry of Susan McCaslin

Susan McCaslin's bright and flowing writing is a series of enactments of her ongoing, deeply felt movements within the intricacies of spiritual awareness. Her prolific forty years of publishing, beginning with her first chapbooks of the mid to late 1970s and continuing with her most recent volumes, amount to a vibrant document of an intense contemplative life. But McCaslin's work is also other and more than this because it is poetry. At its most finely pitched moments, it is poetry that reaches into a unique bliss that dispels conventional religious formulae and gives passionate utterance to what can only be called the energies of love. In its propelled progression, her work breaks all obstacles to establish imaginative freedom and arrive at an open consciousness.

Like her chief literary companions—William Blake and the British Romantic poets, Vernon Watkins, and Denise Levertov—McCaslin's poetry is steeped in the literature of religious wisdom, especially Christian mysticism. As she relates in her 2014 memoir, *Into the Mystic: My Years with Olga*, McCaslin has long engaged in spiritual practice. Her mentor, Olga Park, whose life, teachings, and influence McCaslin details elegantly in that memoir, taught the poet, among other things, "Divinity in the dimmed violet, / Goddess in the sunflower" (from the poem "Dream Cables" in *A Plot of Light*). McCaslin's friendship with Park allowed her to write the following about how she sees the mystic:

> For me, a mystic is a person whose life is an embodiment of love.... A genuine mystic [is] a person whose entire life is moving into alignment with the vast system of nature and the invisible worlds that encompass and transcend those we can

see and measure. A mystic's love begins with the self, the family, the local community, but extends to the planet and even the universe, grounded in an inclusive mystery.

The definition McCaslin offers here can be used to characterize how her work exists in the contexts of both mysticism and poetry. At one point in her memoir, speaking of vivid, vital dreams, McCaslin states, "The original experience seems unspeakable, yet can be companioned by words"; later in the same passage she says, "Language hints at the invisible like footprints in snow"; and finally, "… words are not mere ciphers, since something of the ineffable clings to them." On creativity, McCaslin asks in *Into the Mystic,* "Why is creativity essential to the mystical life?" and answers that for her, "it lies at its very core and is inseparable from empathy and compassion."

To follow McCaslin on the way of her seeking consciousness is to encounter the figure of Jesus, the figure of the sacred female or feminine aspect of God in various guises, the divine lover, beloved, child, and family, sacred entities, and ecstatic visions and mystical experiences that elude words except as imaginative indicators. In addition, McCaslin creates original portrayals of and engages with mythological figures, particularly those in the Demeter and Persephone myth. Teresa of Avila and Thomas Merton provide poetic impetus and inform discrete pieces and poem cycles. McCaslin takes up archetypes of spiritual exploration and enacts them in her poetic enterprises, absorbing these archetypes into her creative life—into levels of herself that touch on the deepest available to us as individuals.

The spirit of William Blake in particular moves through a number of McCaslin's poems. In an early lyric, "A Dream of William Blake" in *Conversing with Paradise* (1986), McCaslin encounters Blake at his artist's easel: "'Sure, my old stuff is fine in its way,' / He said with a sloughing of skin, / Then pointed with flashing hand / To eternity where his new works evolve." By the time of her collection *Locutions* (1995), McCaslin is voicing dynamic and artful invocations of the divine feminine—as if conjuring her own vision of Blake's figure of Jerusalem; in "She Stands at the Mall" McCaslin declares, "She is Wisdom, Hokhmah ... She is God and her hands beseech."

In *Letters to William Blake* (a hand-set collector's edition publication which appeared in 1997 and won the Mother Tongue Press's Annual Chapbook Competition), the poems of which also appear in *The Altering Eye* (2000), McCaslin addresses Blake in letters that competition judge P.K. Page called in her citation "a remarkable series of poems about modern life and its dilemmas," adding that the colloquial tone McCaslin achieved was "both familiar and respectful." "You are," McCaslin says to Blake in "Dear Blake," "the real dream I am interpreted by."

Next to her poems to Blake in *The Altering Eye,* McCaslin includes a cycle of poems about Teresa of Avila. McCaslin addresses the sixteenth century Spanish mystic in pieces distinguished by intensity and insight. This is the closing section of "Interior Castle":

Since you lived in a Medieval walled town,
your soul built you an interior castle

you could not enter
for you were already in it.

You were it, so the speak,
giving us to understand

how many ways there are
of being

in the capacious palace
of the self.

Aspects of the sacred female, "God's exiled female self" and "the Eternal Female in Space," as McCaslin refers to her in "Before the Silver Cord Is Snapped and The Golden Bowl is Broken" and "The Song of the Shulamite" (*Locutions*), appear in the figure of McCaslin's earthly mother in some of her most powerful poems. This is the final stanza of the title poem of *Flying Wounded* (2000):

> The wounded daughter in her mad flight
> from the wounded mother
> holds her heart before her like a crucifix
> and none of them understands how the wound began
> or where its gaping ends.

These are lines from the concluding stanzas of "Getting Religion," a moving examination of McCaslin's mother's psychosis also included in *Flying Wounded*:

> We worry about how much money
> is being diverted into envelopes
> marked "full gospel," how many
> times she lays her hands on the TV
> for healing.
>
> Yet behind all that hype
> is something protecting
> itself in a star net of something
> larger, more loving, something
> that makes me want to call her
> incipient ecstatic …

"What if Demeter," McCaslin asks in her Foreword to *Demeter Goes*

Skydiving (2011) "shook off her ankle bracelets, corn tassels, and garlands, and began a tour of our improbable culture?" With this question McCaslin begins a rich exploration of myth, spirituality, and personal history to produce poetic commentary on a consumerist contemporary world. In the title poem of the collection, Demeter appears in a shopping mall:

> Flanked by milling shoppers
> jockeying for positions in line ups,
> I walk through a labyrinthine, underground mall,
> past elegant makeup counters, robotic joggers,
> into rooms of stockpiled merchandise,
> oil tanks, missiles, endless silent hallways
> that open at last on a corn-yellow room
> where light streams from a skylight
> on the braided head of a woman
> playing a grand piano and singing.

Resonant signature poems start to appear in force and number in McCaslin's work with the beginning of the new millennium. The collections *The Altering Eye* (2000); *Flying Wounded* (2000); *At the Mercy Seat* (2003); *A Plot of Light* (2004); *Lifting the Stone* (2007); *Demeter Goes Skydiving* (a Finalist for the 2012 BC Book Prizes Dorothy Livesay Award and the winner of the 2012 Robert Kroetsch Alberta Book Publishing Award); and *The Disarmed Heart* (2014) show McCaslin exercising strikingly clear poetic prowess. Poems such as "Writing to Magnolia," "Blessed Are the Poor in Spirit," "Wilderness/Poetry," "Migrating into God," "Shame," "Water Corona," "Demeter Goes Skydiving," "Persephone Hears a Layered Singing," "Demeter Pauses at the Foot of the Kokanee Glacier," "When the Stones Rise," and "Living Clothes"—to mention a dozen—mark a poet writing at full powers in her passionate involvement with language and imagination, and integrating roles of poet, mystic, daughter, spouse, mother, and friend under the single, mysterious, awed aegis of the human being. This is from "Water Corona" (*Lifting the Stone*):

> To meditate on water in her many transformations—
> runnel's zest, creek's crouch, waterfall's
> leap, glacier's gathered tears,
> the promises of wells—
> is a privilege of the hydrated,
> but those whose cells pant
> for water's deepest ministry
> cry for a dram to parched throats,
> flow that embraces the human
> and more than human worlds.
> So, it is our luck to contemplate
> the pure springs of dreams,
> to wake, thirsting, fill a glass brim-full,
> enjoy what is not limitless balm.

This is a stanza from "When the Stones Rise" (*The Disarmed Heart*):

> Now is all particular, particularized:
> what the eye sees through you
> and you through the eye, unknown
> a laser sharpening, dissolved
> These bright periwinkles under the window—
> on their exact colour our words may not agree
> Yet outside, rough bark of draughty Douglas fir
> conceals a Persian miniature
> secret calligraphy etched into bark

Distilling words, you open each sound free
projecting pebbles to immensity

McCaslin's imaginative enactments permit us to witness her "migration to God" as she calls it at one juncture in a poem in *At the Mercy Seat* that has that phrase as its title—her "heart afloat / in the wide grey strait / with the wild inland geese." The mundane world with its "busyness" is shot through with signs of a larger, deeper life of delicate beauty, whimsy, ecstasy, and grace. And at all times, the inner core set of notes sounding through her poetry is poignantly personal. This is from "Mindfulness" (*Flying Wounded*):

You cannot know what's coming.
Why arm for disaster?

Disarm, disgrace yourself
if necessary
But be in your place
as the globed magnolia.

You are not the first or the last
to change.

The magnolia flower that appears in "Mindfulness" appears at regular intervals in McCaslin's poetry, from her early work to her very latest, and can be considered a recurring favoured image. Perhaps it is anticipated in "Tree" from her 1979 chapbook, *Kindling*, where the speaker asks that she be "crown[ed]" and that her boughs "wake with dancing flowers":

Pierce, pierce my roots to heaven
Crown me with choiring birds.

Thorn my brow with arcs of fire.
Feed me star-food,
That from this dark and inauspicious shell
My heavy boughs may wake with dancing flowers.

Botanists believe that the magnolia has existed since the beginning of time, and may be the first flower. Thus, the magnolia serves as an emblem of ancient essences, of awareness stretching back to the origins of creation. In "Magnolia Angel" (*Locutions*), McCaslin addresses an angel she observes "compacted in bud / or loosed from the twig / in tincture of rose-to-white / fleshy aromatic petals"; she says, "How easily / you unwing yourself before us." In "Writing to Magnolia" (*At the Mercy Seat*), one of McCaslin's purest lyric pieces, she tells us "She wants" to be loved in a way that W.B. Yeats tells us in his poem "For Anne Gregory" no one could love Anne Gregory—"for herself alone / and not for her yellow or auburn hair" and "that and more...." The poem closes with these stately lines:

That and more:
the mastery in love,
and you, Magnolia,
casting your fleshy dress
like snow at my feet.

The magnolia appears in "Shame" (*Lifting the Stone*): "Outside, the magnolia's unfurling / slims the air / even now uniting the words we are..."; "Here on the lawn, Magnolia, lover, beloved, / shudders to her roots...." It appears in "Language Alive" (*Lineage*): "The language / winks back / running its hands through our hair / through old Magnolia's / thick creamy / petals." In a final permutation the magnolia appears as a chalice in "A Magnolia Chalice for Glenda" (*Lineage*): "Magnolia presence at full flower / lifts into setting sun..."

And so in her most recent collection, as in a compendious imaginative movement, McCaslin's spiritual gaze turns to the magnolia and it becomes her personal chalice. McCaslin states the following in *Into the Mystic*: "What we call God is the Presence that sustains the containment, the containment itself, the shattering of the containment, and what lies beyond the containment. This presence is the Poet, Evolver, Friend who mediates within us, beside us. The containment is alive." Here in the chalice of this elegy for a friend is the poetic containment of the mystical presence.

The "fleshy dress" of the magnolia in "A Magnolia Chalice for Glenda" appears in new form at a "coronation" in the "interior castle" of the self in the marvellously singing "Living Clothes" (*The Disarmed Heart*):

> This unified coronation dons the aquamarine swirling skirt
> which falls over my head, twirls like a carousel
> and plunges into breath   this only ever now

"I fell in love with a forest / and became an activist," McCaslin says in "O Lovers' Tree" (*The Disarmed Heart*). In 2012, McCaslin initiated the Han Shan Poetry Project in support of an old rainforest near her home in Langley, British Columbia. As Mark Hume reported in *The Globe and Mail* in December of 2012, "a legion of Canadian poets [rallied] to save an entire forest grove ... a group of writers ... trying to stop council from selling a ten-hectare parcel of land, by having their poems strung to the trees." McCaslin's activism of recent years has not only moved her to write environmentally conscious poems, but also resulted in political change. Her Han Shan Poetry Project resulted in the Langley Township Council taking the endangered McLellan Forest off the market. It has now been preserved for posterity as the Blaauw Eco Forest.

The mystic, word weaver, and environmental activist were all one from the outset in this poet of spirituality, integrity, and transformation. As McCaslin's work continues through its cycles, she moves at once inward and outward into fuller and fuller consciousness—"into the open." Here, as she puts it in the brief final poem in this *Selected*, "Poem for the Solstice," with its title calling up the changing of the seasons, the turning of Earth, and its play on Hopkins' line about "the world" and "grandeur," "Everything is charged with love."

—Russell Thornton

from **Locutions** *(1995)*

She Stands at the Mall

Face pale and round as the moon.
She is Wisdom, Hokhmah.

There is judgment in her name
but not the kind you expect.

She is God and her hands beseech.
She is woman and she laments

on the hill by the open gate.
She sits like a heron,

pilaster chiselled in dusk.
Displaying herself in the half-light

where people throng to shop
she seems to have something to offer.

She could be a whore
with her heart a sachet of incense

but you have mistaken her again.
She is virgin—not the kind you want.

Distilled, pressed out, she keeps
her power unbroken.

Her eyes are a colour
you have not invented.

They seep from so many places.
She is speaking, appealing.

Listen.
She appeals now to so very few.

I Was Fashioned in Times Past, in the Beginning

Think ballerina stars—
then throw them back into a point.

Think sea—
then meld it to the sun

let it swallow the moon and sun,
let it shimmer as it devolves to mire

and a small sucking sound, a single cell
perfect in its finite way.

Think earth, springs, mountains, hills,
pockets of incensed air, pine needles erect

whirring into a vortex—white dwarf.
Then in that utter silence

long before past was what you call past,
imagine me, leafless, twigless

pregnant with myself,
pregnant within creative spirit

single, before the fecund blast
danced out of the unformed

into what you see—blue camas, manzanitas,
blue-eyed Marys, sea-blush

lavender shooting stars, coral root, orchids—
a thousand islands floating across time.

Wisdom Has Built Her House

The other side of monster-mega-homes
on cramped suburban lots where instant

neighbourhoods arise for instant profit,
Wisdom, with a carpenter's saw and plane

has smoothed her cedar, set cleverness
in the foundation, perspicacity in the frame,

wit in the joins. She has withdrawn
her hands and finished with "a little

night music," installing herself
as she builds out of laughter

a house to outlast times, seasons.
Just outside the strip mall, beyond

the grease of quick burgers and fries,
she has laid her table, spiced her wine.

Before the Silver Cord Is Snapped
and the Golden Bowl Is Broken

remember me. You are facing emptiness
not death. Just what you failed to imagine.

Every snap is a break, luck for you,
if you know how to use it.

The reins at the back of your neck
are silver cords that have rested

in the hands of significant angels.
The bowl that is your body's

deepest thought, empties its wine
beyond grief and beyond measure

where I, God's exiled female self,
catch in my hands your golden secret.

They say you have conjured me
out of dust to palliate despair.

But what is this voice,
draped in the cloth of your being?

Moving More Easily Than Motion,
I Pervade and Permeate All Things

pure decree newly issued from the mouth,
guest resident in pileated woodpecker,

tree frog, bald eagle, Garry oak,
arbutus, island within island dreamed.

And if I hook you by claw or talon,
branch or piercing twig, giving you over

for an instant to the power of right
discernment, a kind of uncommon sense

or skill to walk your sterile streets
or in a guise or mask shaped by me,

the means and end of your walking
will never be separate. The fear

of what you can do or not do
is only the beginning of me.

In My Friendship Is Pure Delight

but despair, inaction, distraction
keep you from clasping my hand,

me from clearing your room
to make a sacred space.

Where in your cheques and balances
is there place for my light

housekeeping, the measureless
spoons of my honey?

The Song of the Shulamite

Nard, myrrh, and cinnamon
drip from my twin-fawn breasts

that have nourished and released
so many star-flung children.

I am swarthy from too much sun
but I have survived trauma.

I have claimed and danced my rage.
I have seen Christ knocking

at the door of the churches
and watched him go away into the night.

I know what it is to stand at a door
pressing the bell to distraction.

I am not an allegory of the bride
though I weave and unweave my veils.

My enclosed garden is not virginity
but a sacred space where I write.

I am sealed off, open only to openness.
I make books and armies

but not for bloody war.
I am Eternal Female in space

but in time I have been both male and female.
When God the Androgyne divides

I and my love rock in volcanic fissures.
His and her answering metaphors

blow the suburbs to smithereens
then to a human shape.

A Garden Enclosed

Faltering into light
the pale green tarragon
mint and reeling lavenders
mouth a honey sun.

Spears of fierce irises
brace for release.
Moribund peonies
sigh magenta rose.

Naked fingers
lift perennial bulbs
brush off flakes of sod.
Push them deeper down

down to rising time.

Summer Reading

Endless summer rain seeps
like indelible white ink
into the spine of a book
open in the middle

just at the place
where the lovers kiss

plummeting past
the indecipherable watermark
their bodies made

where the story's other end
meets the end of the page.

The book goes up—
conflagration fanned to gold.

The lovers are fishing
the book from the stream,
drying its damaged leaves in the sun,
tracing with their salt lips
its broken colophon.

Beloved, Unnumbering the Stars

Who counts
my purse of eggs
my bag of tears
dropping one by one
into time's thicket?

Each egg lost in its tear-pool
each tear circled by its star

I cannot impose my order on the world
or even guide my rich, unnumbered eggs' careen.

Aphoristic Love

My body memorized your body
like the timetables.

My body memorized our body
as if my life depended on it.

O, for a short compendium
of the dreaming body

not for the best
that has been thought and said

but for a short history
of the dreaming, abridged mind

abbreviated for the nonce
like foolscap compressed

into yellow wafers.
One taste, and suburban refugees

might become (if not whole)
at least addicts of the holy.

Magnolia Angel

Astir, compacted in bud
or loosened from the twig
in tincture of rose-to-white
fleshy aromatic petals.

How easily
you unwing yourself before us.
Only a brief fluttering
gives you away.

Human Angel

You are the one who goes and returns
in fire and morning chatter
over oatmeal and newsprint.

In your eye's heart a window
opens and the stars fall in,
periodically disclosing more

comfort than you know, eremite.
You bewilder my wildernesses.
A thousand campanulas ring

tintinnabulation in our small
talk. Solid, you walk beside me
where Thrones, Dominions whirl

our days into an upward vortex
over the iced green grass
and home to our warm bed.

Poetry Angel

The coal has lain
so long on your tongue,
you are fire.

Even in our chill reception
you lay yourself open,
thinking our no longer
private thoughts.

Scarved in colloquies
you unbind yourself—
butterfly-out-of-zinnia.

Someone, somewhere
will write you out,
exhaustless one

recapitulating us
who stammer out your word.

Polysemous Angel

You are the word we most listen for
or do not, the koan we break
our heads against till we plunge
into your garment's flesh and flow.
Come in, please. Give us a definite
yes or no. Mean one and one thing
only. You refuse. But hand out
seamless shrouds we throw and throw off.
Then you dress us in words we must interpret.
Words that slip and slip, growing wings.

Music Angel

You brandish stars, bend spheres.
But who has heard how deeply
you have sunk yourself in sound?

How your love draws our ohs.
Your binding chords, your roping
lines rest, rest and play.

When I was nine you clapped out
the whole of Beethoven's ninth;
cantatas undulated in my head

as if an orchestra had set up.
Once your voice carved chrysolite,
accompanied by a single violin.

Plato said to copy the Forms.
But who could keep your pace?
Only when you mattered inside me

did your music linger, ambrosial.

Evolution Angel

Swinging around this wounded island
earth, she dives at the word

of another, underground where dream
burrows into vision, planting her gifts

in the rooms prepared for her;
cave or tinctured chamber, four

book-lined walls, diamond apex
cut by Spirit's shaft.

Arcs of her feet grip down
into matrix, mother. Stars

shoot in where there were none.
Brain curls round the pearl

that will survive it.

from **Light Housekeeping** (1997)

Time-traveller

Tenuous life within me now,
a pulsing heart without a name,
my galaxy of light in dark,
time casts you on a screen.

Cave-dweller of an ancient clan,
unborn, you sip the milky sea.
Your bright and enigmatic face
has fastened dreams to me.

Sometimes a female, then a male,
I never know when you will sound
your resonating, ancient drum,
Amphitrite's little one.

Somewhere you are complete and whole.
I feel as though we've met before,
dark tumbler tossed and dancing on
Love's lofty sleeping horns.

Fish

You learned to swim before you could breathe,
and now we know that life comes from the sea.
Your animated gills dissolve in light
and soft Pythagorean song.
You made your bodily form
by listening long.

Bull-dancer

Like those acrobats on Minoan walls
posed between eternities in Cretan caves,
Taurean acrobat turns, spins slowly
in a lighter-than-air world.

I could cup her in my hand
(the lids and fingers so delicate)
though her athletic mind has voyaged
from a completeness to this beginning.

Horns of the great bull
are points of contact for her feet.
In innocence and secrecy
she imitates the ancient dance.

Postulates

Fear can destroy
the posture of infinity in the womb,
and the soldier's grave darken
the raptures of birth.

This world is not safe,
though angels' sinews straddle the child.
She will advance by perfect stages
on the old imperfect stage.

Proportions

Narrow as a honeybee
wide as a star,
swinging from small to great
and great to small she knows
mother's milk spills from the galaxy
and (as bee at marigold)
sips at that font.

Forms

The skater's falling figure
turns in air to filigree.

The speaker's lapsing word
becomes a haiku etched on ear.

The lost explorer's pass
becomes through luck an entry place—

the flawless realm
where flaws become the forms.

Woman Dining Alone

Don't mistake her:
she is not lonely scattered over there
with her books and napkins,
not escaping marital dread.

She loves her husband, daughter.
Neither is she on the make
posing with the soup *du jour*
diffident over bread and butter
glancing up to see who is looking
at a woman dining alone.

Eating can be (they say) satisfaction
of animal need, communal act.
Yet this (don't turn your heads
at the arrival of the entree)
this is her hour of repose
between candle and journal,
a savouring of the inner life
that goes on so much of the time
without her.

And if with a fork in one hand
and a pen in the other

she scribbles words in that small black book,
she is not an artiste.
Words too are her nourishment.

The Room of Things Lost

I burst through chilly passages
carried on an updraft
to the room of things lost.

Here space is solid, light a drapery
folded back, and all objects, images
familial, familiar:

my ragged Janey doll,
one black, beloved eye cocked;
my red purse of precious coins

left in a cemetery;
the heart-shaped garnet necklace
lost on campus; the pearl from my husband

slipped from its setting;
treasures warm, as if just unclasped
from neck or hand

all dear gifts, acquisitions grieved,
consigned at last to oblivion.
Who stored them here?

There are other things, not things—
my daughter's unscarred back
before the accident

my father's youthful face,
flushed with well-being,
my childhood faith

after futile search abandoned,
untarnished, mothless
ready for new use.

from **Veil/Unveil** (1997)

"When will the repose of the dead come about
and when will the new world come?"
He said to them:
"What you expect has come, but you know it not."

—The Gospel of Thomas

Persephone

Out of the long blocked dark she trails
behind herself, stepping on ash roses
leaving no impression, impressed by little.

All the burgeoning lilacs and lilies
in the upper world are cool trickles
to which she bends her upward ear,

the dark Lord long erased from her brain,
the frenzied mother, frail and far above
her treading. At this halfway house,

gathering herself for the last ascent,
she will ask no one the way, pause
to touch the snail's small cusp,

the spongy sides of the sleepy sheep
who lost its way going down
the dark, dripping, cavernous stair.

She will not rejoin her mother this year
or return to the dark king who scooped
her body up so many turns of the earth.

She will (at the risk of disappointing
or seeming rude) remake her myth
as the seasons rotate without her.

Just the Other Night

I saw Jesus, Buddha, and Mohammed
on a tufted slope overlooking a city
which could have been Jerusalem but was not,
sharing a coffee in brown stoneware mugs
they had ground from earth's sweet coffers.

And none of them was preaching or arguing
with the other about anything
because they were tracking the course
of a small black ant struggling
to attain a crest of its choosing.

How to help without interfering
was all their talk,
and admiration of the rich soil
which cupped them all like unbroken shards
against a sea-dropped sky.

Holy, Holy, Holy

Why three holinesses? Earth, sky
and the whole that holds them in
one staggering breath. All is hale
hagiography somewhere, but here
"the broken rounds," said Browning.

And even in this wild geography
of snapped synapses, the mouth
forms its ahs before the pert
fullnesses of robins, and the
demented fullness of a woman

who pauses in her anxiety to
observe and listen to the most
high, most high, invading
her chatter, calming her dark
Lenten bones. Here in its knitting

She-Spirit weaves coverings,
hovers thrice holy.

Blessed Are the Meek

if you mean the humbled
before starfish in starscape
blessed are the dumbfounded
by robust organic wheels
that move us round
what star our centre moves

if you mean those who are inexpressibly happy
in lush peonies' breath, the waft
of mock orange wearing white shoulders

       but not if you mean humble pie deference,
       the predicted suburban round, smoothing
       the edges of male ego's rub.

Let us be voiceless before honeybee's prelude
mouthed in roses,
not silenced by fear or diffidence.

Let us be mothers or not mothers
in our own ways and times.

Blessed are the lambs
for their union with grass and herb,

and cursed be the meekness that hides
and bends and quenches its own fire.

>   So do not ask
>   the ravaged and defoliated,
>   to forgive their accusers and abusers
>   when it is they who need
>   that admonishment.

For blessed (not merely happy)
are the emptied
of what they thought themselves
for they shall inherit all
the lovely earthen things

that they are, and sky as well.

Conch

The word is curved and round
like a roseate couch
where delicate, racy Aphrodite
might have reclined with Mars;
a seaflower for her quiet
stepping into the world

an evolved and elongated ear
turned inside out
for the reception
of Siren's reedy song.

It is my daughter's pink bedroom
winding up into
a mysterious passage
to dark and darker pink,
so fleshy and pure
it will set her out gently
among the stars
that give but do not take
her small light.

Dancing at Long Beach

She fawn-steps and twirls
in fermenting light
mimicking some nimble-footed
mermaid's return from the sea.

Her hair is a sheath of amber
burning down her back.

She flings the fine sea mud,
pounds the turf with fierce wild toes.

Then all her seven years
bend to kiss the re-enchanted shore.

Called away
she finger traces, "I love you, sea,"
on clean canvas
repeating what her dance had already spoken.

From a Galilean Poet

The wind blows in
wherever there's an opening for it,
and you haven't got a clue where
it comes from or where it's heading.

Don't be surprised if I say you've
got to be born into that wind-world.
Call it above, or call it within;
imagine there's a cave you're crawling out.

And the wind-born will be twice born
but not from belief or theology,
an emotional trip or slogan
to stick on your bumper.

For God's sake, we're talking life,
we're talking poetry, something
larger moving through
that sings in the veins.

from **Into the Open** (1999)

Hymn to the Holy One

Holy One, with your star-lined face,
your deep remoteness, even your terror,
we praise you for you intimate grace,
your falling with the lonely sparrow.

We praise your entrance into sound,
for matter's secrets, still unknown.
We praise your globe, still turning round
that brings us closer to your throne.

We praise your laws, inward and right,
built into every living thing.
They draw us nearer to your light
and help us hear the Muses sing.

Tales of your wrath are overwrought.
Your absence is our only hell.
Trees of your planting, we the sought,
know patient nurturing makes us well.

You are the Seeker and the Will;
we find you in our deepest core,
and yet beyond. We cannot kill
the love that leaves us wanting more.

We picture you with whitened strands,
Ancient of Days, a holy King,
and yet you show a mother's hands,
immanent, yet transcendent being.

We praise your realized Word, the One,
however known, by whatever name,
and us the seedlings love has sown
through sacrifice and human pain.

Come now and enter in our hearts.
Our need is mutual and the same;
your whole repeated in our parts,
our guardian Spirit, sustaining flame.

Muse's Coda

Building with words is my way,
till words translate to acts
acts to words, and words again to silence.

Because it is impossible
to imagine endless duration,
I speak from particular places.

Eternity is a many-mouthed river,
a field for the plowing,
a music in the lotus of the heart.

We are separate; we are one
in alternating rhythms.
Creator—creature, I help you create.

Because you approach the world
through words and images,
I lead you to places of silence.

I ask persons of deeds
to make themselves my book
and read that script.

Wherever I work,
wherever you hear my voice
is the kin-dom, within, without.

I shatter all your categories.
I am ruthless but kind—
the kindly light unfolding from a seed.

from **The Altering Eye** *(2000)*

The eye altering, alters all.

—William Blake, from "The Mental Traveller"

William Blake, Esquire, Eternity

Dear Sir,
Mr. Blake,

Yo Blake! (erase.)

Look, there's no one around
here like you to talk to and having
admired (scratch), "relished" your verve
so long and being long past graduate school
I just want to say from this shoulder
of North America out of the nine-month
Vancouver rainy season, fatigue,
and Ulro that I am ready to look
within the sandgrain, harsh, unrefractive,
and build what I can, something new, that is
with your kind assistance Mr. B., please.

Otherwise the grains fly back in my face.

Yrs,

Dear William

So if your Dad beat you for seeing your tree full of angels
What of us who got TV instead of Vision and no beatings?
What happens to the reconstructive Imagination
after a hundred replays of *I Love Lucy*
or driving down the Information Highway
or thousands of hours in front of Nintendo?
Not part of your cosmology?
You wouldn't rant?
Go ahead and blast the stations of the nerves alive
with jumping words.

Look, I just require an hour
away from the mechanical ratio
of laundry and driving my child to lessons,
a tall decaf latte at Starbucks.

But then I'm back in it
and it's all monotony again.

Please pass me down a sunflower
rooted in its orbit round the sun.

Ah, Sunflower!
I cling to your roots
while dangling over the abyss.

Yrs,

Dearest William

When you turned a guinea an inch or so wide
into a host of heavenly angels singing Holy
Holy Holy by looking not with but through
the eye, did you float upward with that look?
Did you enter your studio singing?
My sun is veiled today but I think she
is a living woman, a female Los,
or Sol spelled backward.

Everything or something speaks
over the Port Moody oil refineries,
a moody place indeed here in the west,
but not unconnected to that England
where Jesus walked out of space
before your nation became nation
and later needed a revolution.

Don't give up on the alarms—
the wake up calls.
Some of us can almost hear you way out here.
Even zombies can turn and turn again,
spinning off their mechanical wheels
and the ratio of their five senses.

Yrs,

Hi Blake

Forgive the tone of false familiarity,
but I dreamed you again so you seem familial,
brotherly, fatherly, motherly maybe.
How is wife Catherine this morning?
Are you still teaching her reading and watercolours?
Is she still insanely jealous of your "lovely rose tree"
(another woman perhaps?) or has she awakened into her own
spring?

More to the point, does she still bring your tea?
On the subject of women, what was all that stuff
about the non-existence of the "female will" in eternity
as if we weren't supposed to have them?
Even Enitharmon, the bride, was an emanation
belonging inside her partner Los, stuck
to her weaving. Sure, it's a noble, feminine
sort of craft worthy of Homeric goddesses,
but couldn't she play Jesus the Imagination too?

In the end you made lovely Jerusalem powerful
and God, him-herself an Androgyne embracing
their coequally eternal bodies. So,
given the playfulness of the gender wars,
if you were to be born again
would you be willing to try it as a woman?

Yours most respectfully,

Dear Will

How did you keep going on your real work
without getting published? I know a few
worshippers came round and started a club
when you were 70, but that's belated praise.
Here you are bent over your illuminated plates,
totally obsessed. I love you
for that and the neat script that just
keeps the images fountaining
in golds and pastel blues, yellows like daffs,
electric fire—unpatented, original, radical
as geodes cracking up
spilling their diamond innards.

Love,

Dear Wm.

Excuse what seems a flippant, irreverent form of address,
but being as you are now, one of the immortals,
I feel you near as my jugular sometimes,
and since you have entered my dreams, setting up
thick canvases and dreamy watercolours,
I risk adopting you as a familiar.
Sometimes your adroit fingers pinpoint something
on my map of Port Moody and arise querulous.
For instance, even coming from your "chartered
Thames," you were appalled at the foul
effluent in the stream near my house.
I can't make it go away just by looking at it
differently, or writing a poem, though I am sure
poetry and language are transformative.
It's the prophet of justice I call for in you
with voice and vision and bright acts
to get inside me (us)
till the waters tumble clear.

Hopefully,

Dearest Blake

I can't help altering your salutation;
yet you seem so namelessly
fierce, it is impossible to settle on just one.
I'll stick with B. for now.

I see the Satanic Mills of pre-industrial London,
children caught on wheels screaming,
and the white female hands lifting and pulling
all day in mechanical rounds.

But have you seen the clear cuts?
Maybe somewhere up there you've met Emily Carr
and wandered her secretive, mossy forests,
the velvet-antlered limbs of her cedars
or traced the shapes of her austere totems.

Imagine, if you will, gigantic terrific machines
descending on whole sides of verdurous mountains
and these mechanical mega-ants, as it were,
razing thousands of living pines and firs
till nothing is left but rapine—balded, scalped
waste, Urizenic wasteland
and utter desolation.

My frail house lies on the edge of this desert.

Yrs truthfully,

Dearest Will

I love your rebel Jesus, unchaste,
insolent to authority and humble to God,
a rabble-rousing friend of whores and thieves,
strung between thieves, but not for long;
romping tygerlimbed out of the desert.

Who would want him for a Church's hero?
No institutional figure—too wild.
Imagine him inside us bursting up like field lilies
each spring, redolent of rage and weeping and poetry.
God for the godless.
I love the way you took him off the cross
and made him a Glad Day,
how you put back all those portions of
sleeping humanity inside us

where they always were.

Lovingly,

Dear Blake

This is just adios and not good-bye
as the song says. When I fling you behind
you rise human from stone.

These popping daffs, lay flowers,
come becomingly in the womb of God
who concurrently enters us
on our evening perambulations
through the burbs.

The long occult sun shows gold,
archaic, robust. After three straight
months of mooning rain,
earthen joys, even slugs
glitter and my blonde cocker's
tail bops recklessly up and down mown lawns.

Accept this slight homage
bandied through air and grammar.

Even out of Ulro I am to you
a sleeper rubbing her eyes
through a crack of day. You are
the real dream I am interpreted by.

Send more briefings for paradise;
keep me informed through the sieve of your eye.

Yrs,

I Have a Few Words to Say to the Freudians

Teresa, that patron saint of hysterics.
                    —Sigmund Freud

about the event in my story
referred to as the "Transverberation,"

the "flaming heart" Crashaw in his poem
got so worked up over 200 years later.

I mean, that angelic piercing,
those darts of core-driven light

all that fusion of pleasure and pain.
You might as well know

there are some ecstasies
having little to do with sex

though we steal whatever analogies we can,
and sex is sometimes a whisper

of what I'm talking about.
Erotics within erotics

bodies in bodies, sheaths in sheaths,
touches of union everywhere so delicate

they imprint the soul with longing.
Yes, there are sublimations, Freud,

having nothing to do with repression,
as the open mouth and the half-closed eyes

of the Bernini in Rome only half suggest.
But you have to try them to know them.

Your Metaphors Aren't Allegories, Teresa

For from those Divine breasts, where it seems that God is ever sustaining
the soul, flow streams of milk, which solace all who dwell in the castle.
                                        —Teresa of Avila, *Interior Castle*

for they just won't serve a teaching,
any teaching,

despite the theologians'
and even your own bold frames.

Silkworm spins out of its crystal palace,
utters and is air.

Christ enters the room
without using a door.

Gender explodes, metaphors meld,
as bridegroom receives the bride

offering her his milky breasts.
But one thing is sure—

all is effortless as the core.
Further down and in

the waters well up
borne without buckets

or handles.

Nothing Is Too High or Low for Your Attention, Teresa

plover, magpie, eagle, gull,
silkworm, hedgehog, tortoise
(graces in hiding),
hare bopping off into intoxicated meadow
butterfly, fledgling hawk,
trillium and clover intertwined like lovers
the plain and the rare,
coarse and rarefied air
infused indescribable white
and the blue-black pits of despair.

Healing Succulent

If when I'm in prayer or on the days in which I am quiet and my thoughts are on God, if all the learned men and saints in the world were to join together and torture me with all the torments imaginable, and I wanted to believe them, I wouldn't be able to make myself believe that these things came from the devil, for I cannot.

—Teresa, *Life*

St. Joseph and our Lady
laid a golden collar on your neck.

You polished Christ
in the mirror of your soul.

You had fruition of each other
in the deepest silence.

Today you could dismiss these
as weird and wacky dreams,

head off for work,
tell your shrink or women friends,

be labeled slightly quirky,
at worst, end up in a mental ward,

or maybe persist
to write, paint, dance them out.

It broke your heart when they
made you snap your fingers at the visions,

dismiss them as naughty brats,
dangerous imps.

Images boiled over the pot
and spilled on the floor.

Jesus told you even then it was tyranny
to expect you to deny them.

But when you defended yourself,
they charged you with pride, *superbia,*

changing things, upsetting the order.
Active mystic, mystic activist,

what politicized you
out of distress into laughter?

You, aloe,
little healing succulent in a dry land.

Paradise Feast

You look on one another face to face, as two lovers do.

—Teresa, *Life*

O, the favours love gave me with Love,
all my little peccadilloes vanquished.

Love made me a warrior for love,
and even Juan de Yepes

(to you, St. John of the Cross),
confrere, younger brother

who wrote so eloquently
of that long embrace

and did his stint in prison too,
sucked from those luxuriant breasts,

wound in his hands
braid of the beloved,

wed in the secret chamber.
We who are in love

sing in the great breath
and counter-breath, yoked coplas,

(and I with so little theology)
breaking forth.

Interior Castle

I can find nothing with which to compare
the great beauty of a soul and its great capacity.
—Teresa, *Interior Castle*

Yet you do, Teresa, compare that is,
prizing analogies, orient pearls,

diamonds, crystals, scented gardens,
even the dry little shrub

palmetto, with its layered rinds
and sticky sweet edible centre.

All things spacious, ample,
small, intricate and precious.

Since you lived in a Medieval walled town,
your soul built you an interior castle

you could not enter
for you were already in it.

You were it, so to speak,
giving us to understand

how many ways there are
of being

in the capacious palace
of the self.

Here on Vancouver Island, Teresa

The silkworms feed on the mulberry leaves until they are full-grown, when people put down twigs upon which, with their tiny mouths, they start spinning silk, making themselves very tight little cocoons, in which they bury themselves. Then, finally, the worm, which was large and ugly, comes right out of the cocoon a beautiful white butterfly.... So now if no one had ever seen this, and we were only told about it as a story of past ages, who would believe it?

—Teresa, *Interior Castle*

the little blue and white larvae
have spun themselves asleep and awakened

already fluttering against the lapping shore.
Your world so dry, and mine so wet.

If a pod of orcas should pass the point,
who would believe it?

For these things move as in a dream
turned slowly inside out.

I am here on retreat:
triathlon of eating, sleeping, reading,

not a reformed life really, not escape,
but a kind of yearly yearning

for something approaching contemplation.
I wonder why you chose for your daughters

such a strictly cloistered life?
More rigour? Self-discipline?

No. A way free from the everyday noise
that distracts psyche's paradise ear.

The spurt and shock of visions
are easy, Teresa,

So how does one distinguish
a transcendent moment with a tulip

or a sixties' LSD trip
from your kind of rapture?

You say a true locution
brings tranquility,

certainty, is unexpected
As egret at dawn, un-induced

Feels more like listening
Than composing.

One has no choice
but to attend.

And it issues finally in good fruits
(palmetto, pear, or plum).

I nestle into dream,
hear the glide of your golden pen

await the unimaginable wings
that will carry me back into the world.

Incarnation

Begin with the fluid body
delicate golden pear
couched in its first cradle
flung from its star

This deep cavity
where the heart thuds in dark
sets out on the nomadic road
wanting it all

a dromedary carrying its water inside

Whale Dream

She presses her hands against the aquarium glass
while a baby whale eases out of the womb space.

She saw it all once on TV before it died,
could not survive in that aquamarine tub.
The mother aimlessly circled her grief.

This one is white, surely a beluga,
and shoots straight into her arms,
imprinting on her face, now stamped for love.

She is impressed with all that blundering style
and lets it follow her everywhere.

On the other side of the Plexiglas
in the swim, she is the mother now,
heaves ashore onto a seaweed couch
where the little one bounces on her stomach.

They are amphibious, comfortable in both worlds
skipping from air to water to air
even as the child grows and grows

spouting language from its sleek head.

The Owl and the Mouse

She is dreaming she is a small creature
swift and fragile
locked to earth's giant bones
snug in long tunnels—
a plain grey field mouse.

Out of the hunting wind,
imperious swoop and wing-span,
terrible, wider-than-God eyes
beautiful brown-shadowed moon face
of the owl with her ruffled feathers
floating down nearer and nearer

where she, terrified and in love,
opens herself in a sacrifice of delirium
to the narrowing space between them.

Lying with My Head in the Lap of the Beloved

pretending to be asleep
but really, listening to the rise
and fall of my breath
the rise and fall of the breath of the beloved.

I do not want to wake
or pretend to wake
for fear of breaking the woven spell
that holds us in one long strand of silk.

I do not know or care to know
if the beloved senses I am here
listening, attentive as a dove
to that breath, rising, falling.

Oracular Heart

Here, in the heart of her nesting
a fawn-and-white rat dandles ten babies
from multiple Diana breasts,
their bare skin pinker than spring salmon.

As they root like tiny blind pigs
deep in the pine chips, she licks
and strokes and covers and warms—
a real working mom who has
adopted some strays besides her own.

Her younglings could fit easily
into the palm of your hand,
their feet transparent as shells.
The mother herself is a child.

Her keepers had not separated her
from her siblings before she was weighty with life.

Shamanic eyes bead from her head
as she climbs and reclimbs
the ladder that leads from treadmill
to sleep's nocturne.

Pegasus

There in the pendulum of my brain, cupped
in your hands, Pegasus comes hurtling
across an electric blue field

surely Pegasus, foam white, head on,
fetlock rippling. Wide-apart eyes
and the undulating wings behind
simply an extension, soft oarings
of the muscled withers

caught in my forehead's covert
all in an instant.

Some practice torture,
some bliss.

I choose Pegasus
that wild stallion
of poetry.

from **Flying Wounded** *(2000)*

The psychology of creativity is in its essence feminine
because the creative world of art leaps forth from the unconscious
depths, that is, from the domain of the mothers.

—C.G. Jung

Next to New

for my mother Phyllis McCaslin, 1921-2003

Second hand rose,
how can I un-forget
the Next-to-New Shop
where you gather cartloads
of variegated garments
in your rounded arms,
drape them over me,
young Persephone
to your dark Demeter?

I want matching cashmere
sweater sets like my friends'
and a pleated skirt
with cheerleader socks
but you fix me up
with '40s-style sweetheart
sweaters and long straight shifts
completely the wrong colours.
Never mind, you can dye them
to match in our archaic washer.

Then you jag my bangs two inches
above my brows, thin them relentlessly,
shouting, "too thick, too thick!"

Our voices shrill behind coat racks
the day I vow I will disown you,
your clothes; cast off
these castoffs forever
and never let you touch
my panoply of hair.

Frogs with Sequined Eyes

Nine stone frogs "ribbit" in the garage
awaiting the sea-foam unbottled paint,
the scarlet and sapphire sequins
she plants on unembellished eyes.

One day she lowers them,
immobile, to the receiving earth
where they sink, settle
near our stumbling threshold.

Neighbors do not ask
about the amphibian dark
or the artisan hands
that horned and spotted them.

Still they leap, leap
under the princely moon
rewriting their transformations
on the breath of her pacing.

Triolet for the Amphetamine Afflicted

"Dear Dr. Hormone feed me for my dinner
those little pills so slippery and so cool.
Just jazz me up; I want to be a winner.
Dear Dr. Hormone feed me for my dinner
those little pick-me-ups that make me thinner.
You know I used to think I was a fool
till Dr. Hormone fed me for my dinner
those little pills so slippery and so cool."

Devil's Eyes and Voices

One day she is reading the Bible
and all the pertinent texts
raise themselves in yellow light;
filaments of words grow fat with meaning
and a fleshy wing circumscribes her
like a wind. There is a whirring
and she rolls like Ezekiel on her side
acting God's rejection and love for Israel.

Her teenage daughter enters the room
wearing emerald eye shadow slanting up
at the corners. Green eyes smirk.

It's the devil wearing green,
old fool, and her daughter has been
whisked away on a wing and a prayer.

The voices begin chanting ditties,
issuing commands; the television
becomes vatic; ubiquitous eyes
murmur threats and promises.

She is finally at the centre of a world.

Catatonic

After the messaging
insidious TV
the men in the wires
outside your window,
the refrigerator who
(austerest god)
commanded worship
on the groveling floor
at 2 a.m., the rummaging
cupboards, the flying
locusts with their stinging tails

you dissolve yourself perfectly
into transparency.
Things lose their long malevolence
as you attain stasis,
invisibility

and for one moment
the devils envy you
with your husband and children
crouched at your knees
calling your name.

You have no name
and so the white jackets come
and give you a wrist-tag
carry you away
to asylum, Elysium.

The Rending

My mother rent her flesh. What did her in?
She didn't want to talk or face the wall.
They shut her in a cell and made her grin.
She couldn't eat; she knew her words were small.
She placed her knife and fork with ritual ease.
A black straw for the bad, a white for good;
Unsmiling, joyless Jesus was a tease
who tripped her up; at last she understood
drumming at heaven's gate long before noon
that he must cast her back to do her duty.
"Go serve your family, you're here too soon."
She wrapped herself in scarves, shed her beauty,
till her lost body, strangely light and fine,
sagged like grey laundry hanging from a line.

Getting Religion

It has always been there—
that soul-deep old-time religion.
The psychiatrist blames her psychosis
on being born in the Bible belt.
For years she modernized, adopted
the skepticism of her college profs;
yet when Kennedy died she compared him
to Lincoln, then to God.

Now she is saying God-light has
permuted the fissures of her brain.
She refuses to appear for therapy,
refuses to converse with
the Freudian who wants to blame
everything on her mother;
swishes her medication
decisively down the toilet
because Jesus is her medico,
her head honcho.

She pipes in radio preachers—
Brother Shamrock from down South
still bellowing the Word on tapes
even after his death; hangs out

in charismatic coffee houses
swaying back and forth to "Jesus
Is a Soul Man" and "Rock-a My Soul."

We worry about how much money
is being diverted into envelopes
marked "full gospel," how many
times she lays hands on the TV
for healing.

Yet behind all that hype
is something protecting
itself in a star net of something
larger, more loving, something
that makes me want to call her
incipient ecstatic, struggling
outside, not merely cracked.

Flying Wounded

The wounded mother flies out of sepia dreams
with the wound seeping just under her breast.
Umbilical twists in its shroud,
falls at the feet of the wounding grandmother
who will not fix her teeth
whose breath stinks
who no longer cares about her appearance
lets appearances go
gave over caring at forty
in her scarves and flowing robes.

The wounded queen mother laughs but cannot love
yet loves in her way, once telling
the wounded daughter, "You are
remarkable, a remarkable woman."

The wounded daughter in her mad flight
from the wounded mother
holds her heart before her like a crucifix
and none of them understands how the wound began
or where its gaping ends.

Rules for Writing Out the Dark

When there is no opening,
no orifice except what you would imagine
if you could imagine sun,
yourself whole, siphoning honey

absolutely, do not
summon spectres,
scare yourself to death.

When angel wings desert stone
and your heart is a flat vibrating stone,
idle dumb tongue,

refuse (absolutely) to replay
the tabloids' desolations.

Instead, breathe light.

Let it in, well in.
Catch sparks on the tip of your pen
and throw them high
past the closed intent of your quarters.

Make windows where no windows were.

Improbably Light

In uncertainty, the middle of,
the living one shows herself crosswise
Joy

The cross's only crux—
rood into goldenrod.

A woman with her
head in her knees
parsed by light.

Her angel flexes.
Love and fear divorce.

Mindfulness

You cannot know what's coming.
Why arm for disaster?

Disarm, disgrace yourself
if necessary
But be in your place
as the globed magnolia.

You are not the first or the last
to change.

Christmas Poem

Out of the deer-stepping wild
one of the moss-tipped tribe stole
wings, swallowed light, flew higher
than any had flown from that wood,
un-barren, singing, married the land
and became bridal sheath, wholly apparent,
appareled, white as a wand,
found the babe, unwrapped and parsed her
to the world all without dividing
a single hair.

from **Common Longing** *(2001)*

Perhaps over all there is a great motherhood, as common longing.

—Rainer Maria Rilke, from *Letters to a Young Poet*

Martha and Mary

As Jesus and his disciples were on their way, he came to a village where a woman named Martha opened her home to him. She had a sister called Mary, who sat at the Lord's feet listening to what he said. But Martha was distracted by all the preparations that had to be made. She came to him and asked, "Lord, don't you care that my sister has left me to do the work by myself? Tell her to help me!" "Martha, Martha," the Lord answered, "you are worried and upset about many things, but few things are needed—or indeed only one. Mary has chosen what is better, and it will not be taken away from her.
—Luke 10. 38-42, New International Version

Martha wipes from the ledge
fine dust through which Mary sees
the world; moving, motioning, fixing,
she steps staccato across time

efficient, neat, always cleaning
behind someone, arranging order
and the satisfaction of things
in their places—nothing out of place.

Mary visualizes. Deserting time
for the ordonnance of space,
summons a garden to dream
or a secret glade to be.

Together they sit or move, move
or sit in a kind of ageless dance,
Martha clearing the path—
Mary riding on her white horse.

Mary and Martha

Martha minds the child,
wipes rice flung on floor and cupboard,
dances attendance on unexpected houseguests,
keeps guard over her tongue while
the microwave beeps—one, two, three.

Mary is upstairs in her study
composing poems into the personal computer—
freeing unicorns and roses from the machine.
They leap like sheep over a stile
and fly out the window over suburban lawns.

Mary and Martha battle for ascendancy
within the woman who sits,
rises, bears some other name.
Sometimes they converse—

then the woman in her dreams hears news—
larger rhythms of the sun and moon.

Another Thing Needful

Marys and Marthas multiply.
They are dancing, their ancient robes
and Israelite features falling away,
melding into lineaments of contemporary women,
shopping, banking, teaching, trading,
touring, selling, buying, giving

not the dreams of men but of themselves.
They are dreaming themselves free.

Flawless Mirror

Mary and Martha meet and embrace
on a ground of white fleurs de lis.

It is Christmas, and the lilies
are dishevelling their petals in white fields.

You say, lilies in winter?
But this is imagination and the world

alters with the altering eye.
So it is Christmas and Martha

is arranging Mary's hair in gold coils.
No aureoles surround them but the light is gold.

And there is a shy bird, perhaps a sparrow,
flickering in and out of the room.

Then together they lift the great glass—
flawless speculum of the active power.

from **At the Mercy Seat** *(2003)*

This cathexis between mother and daughter—
essential, distorted, misused, is the great unwritten story.

—Adrienne Rich, from *Of Woman Born*

White Meditation

Begins as a humming behind the ear,
a musical mood, dark listening.

Meaning thrums, circles, intends
toward us, tends us well.

Why bother to arrest
that unlovely, unlikely suspect

of a thought? I'm no cop.
Let it go by. All strictures die.

Loop your skittish will
to the wild horsewoman.

Lasso yourself to the subtle stars
which are not fixed, glued.

Drop the priest and magus,
become the hermitess

small, brown and peripheral,
an effective nobody

in rainforest or desert
an occasion for speech, or silence.

When the world speaks
try not to get in the way.

A Blank Slate

Try to be a sheet of paper with nothing on it.
                                    —Rumi

1

Step on the tiles in cold, bare feet.
Kiss the words flying.

Letters in the updraft whirl,
savour of some unsung alphabet.

2

Something rises to the top.
Again, the poem is writing itself
with or without you.

No more willing it.
You are a handful of cinnamon
flung in the pot,
a sprinkling of yeast in the dough.

3

Exhale yourself in a breath of steam.
Inhale the world at your door:

fresh February snows on Burke Mountain,
quilt of kisses drawn
over a slumbering child.

4

The world will always be larger
and you will die into it (late or soon)
peering from a kitchen window
where the white hawthorn
preps for its own Spring term.

5

Grant yourself one mantra of breath
deep in the lungs.
Fast-walk from the suburbs of the body
to the fringing hills.

Dogs in short sweaters are there before you
nursing within themselves
the buried howl.

6

Stepping into the fluorescent Safeway air,
buy peppers—green, red and yellow.

Bring them home, cross-section them,
feed them to your loved ones in salad or pasta.

Clean up.
Lay out your books and pens on the table.
Be consoled,
consumed by the blank page.

7

This body's music:
footprints of tiny sparrow's
fretwork in the hills.

8

Midnight, your head is on the lap of the beloved.
The beloved knows
you are only pretending to be asleep,
listening to that breath
rising, falling.

Cariboo Rain

With signs of dryness everywhere—
incense air
scrawny lodge pole pines dripping needles
and erect brown-topped firs

the two-week rain comes as a boon
forcing us to the cabin
to stretch and catnap
and walk out at last
after a week of doing nothing

into the ruby gloss of rosehips
spread across the road,
the moony brown-eyed-Susans
and mauve daisies
tipsy in their twirl.

Silence to Wrap My Sleep Around

Something arises or is given,
grace in the mind and across the page

seabottle, something with echo of sea,
clear and subtle, caught in a sidelong glance.

Looked at the wrong way, it skitters off.
Heart heaves back in the chest.

Lyric incapacity to sustain the gift,
keep it up and moving.

Effort loses; attention brings it back
as silence wraps it round.

Out of that sleep, what linens,
beads and relicts fall?

Unwrapped, rapt,
wiser than snow.

Less a eureka moment
than a white flutter behind the ear.

No Fear

The angel's first words are always,
Fear not, fear not, Mary.

And in the holy now kin-dom
no fear mongers or anxious ones,

not because anyone is excluded,
but because fear casts us from our deep selves.

Most of our lives a fending off of phantoms
who if they come, are not as they seem.

How many dreams a prospect of emptying,
falling, waking out of terror?

How many deaths a passport to somewhere
unimagined?

Elder Brother

Jesus, who could bear to be you,
carving out centuries with your metaphors—

buried pearls, cryptic, enigmatic tales,
your ragtag band of fishermen and thieves?

Little you care whether we remember you
as human or God. All that prickly disputation.

Your kin-dom is still a child,
something lost and found.

Non-violent, yet such a guerrilla
you got yourself killed,

knew what that flattening death meant,
a showdown on a field, a sign.

To live like a field lily, springing back—
a few have done it.

Liberation

(on *Liberation* by F. H. Varley)

[You] can embody truth but [you] cannot know it.
—W.B. Yeats

Here, in the hive of our days,
you have left us an open door,
someone walking out of light
so dazzled it breaks to blue green rose.

Matter too has changed
and the possibilities of flesh,
flayed, splayed, now
like an open palm, unnailed.

Here, now, we are that person
walking in, that being
walked into, a presence
in the part that vivifies.

Someone has entered
and overleapt the self to return
and say with all colours:
this body, it is good

as we glide through the door
of ourselves where honey globes,
dripping like streaks of paint
onto our hands, feet, tongues.

In this place and this crowning,
the box we once thought large enough
has broken like a lime sarcophagus.
We are liminal, and literal, and walking.

Panorama Ridge

Lush tangle of wet cedar bones,
moist embrace of licking ferns,

graceful, up to our heads,
rippling heat through nine kilometers

of switchbacks high to succulent
alpine meadows where we couple

under blue stars. Our breaths conspire
against mosquitoes and black flies

bouncing like raindrops on a pup tent
made for one. Eighteen years ago

we bonded in a tent. Now rejoining,
our tongues sing a bush fire

quenched by lupine, heal-all, fireweed,
blown anemone, white heather

and the mild rein orchid.
We are brown marmots, camouflaged,

khaki lovers anointing our lost, found flesh
for the steep descent, and long glissade home.

Contemplation

Accustomed to distraction
somehow I fell into a sacred space,
template awaiting its musical score
(myself devoid of music)

A robin in the rain
could have told me
in the streaked grey
all was silent

Water splashed in a pond
like words around their hush.

Into the Whirlwind

How long till the woman of sorrows enters the whirlwind of the
striped tulip, whirlwind of the hummingbird's wing? How long
till she lodges between the redwood's bark and its sap, till a
woman of no blame dances where Leviathan and Behe-
moth are two prongs of one dilemma, plunging deep-
er into the oven of bliss where Goddess wrestles her-
self for a blessing suffering beside us inside the
wronged tree through a tornado of bliss
and bane then blazing in the dark
whooshing spiral of the peacock's
eye or in the chittering chim-
panzee dark? How long till
the saint is spit from
the dragon's eye
and the seed
lets itself
fall

open,
till the
engorged
sky empties its
wealth of rain on
the prophet's wind-
stirred head? How long
till the Magdalen undoes her
hair and Christ blazes in the sev-
ered amoeba brain? How long till the
toes and fingers trace riddling words, till
the books fling out their stories of healing and
the nesting tables of the soul set out the only food.
How long till Jahweh's entering Job is Job's entering Jahweh,
till periphery and centre merge again till the closed cubicles
release their honey and the wild wolves play tug-of-war in gentleness?

Christ Meets Eve in the Underworld

The harrowing road he runs along
leads him at last to wetland greenery
drenched in a lifeless hail of grey,
where she, our first Mother, clothed
in a dress of pomegranate flame
scrapes away the moss and leaves
that stop an underground stream.

Her eyes, lighting on the tall stranger,
brim tears at his words: *Ave, Eva*—
greeting material, germane.
She scoops some water into a ladle
and lifts it to his lips: *How is it you come*
so late to this dim vestry, dragging
words as from a lost domain?

Depth of Earth, you who took the blame
before the loss of paradise,
take from me now this massive crucifix
and let me bend my will to yours
releasing all your wilderness
into the mechanical cities.

Together they weave a spiritual body,
cut a window in the forehead
for the oasis of visions,
and set a door-harp in the cavity
where once an ailing heart had lain.
Through the mouths of creatures
flies the immanent Jesus-Mother

skimming into the world she had never left.

The Omnipresence of Moss

The Cauldron Mother rolled it from her apron
patting it into a damp, spongy ball,
then laid it among triads of hemlock, cedar, fir,
flinging it at last into the orbit of Uranus

where it magnified itself in unstoppable green,
tufting and clustering in decay,
cryptogamous, keeping from everyone
the spores of its hidden marriage.

Had the Mother chosen Mars, that armed
red planet might have renounced war
and all its trouble, for green carries
such softness to the eyes.

Even in this West Coast neighbourhood
no herbicide can keep it from wrapping itself
around the tree trunks, stones, and the crevices
of my misty March garden.

Again and again it lowers itself to places
below our feet, offering itself to weary heads
in all its myriad shades of green
and in all the drenched names of green.

All I would ask now is a chaise longue of mosses,
just for a few moments to be pavilioned
close as stone to moss.

A Flying Dream After Ten Years' Grounding

How often I used to dream
the rotary buzz of wings,
small nubs tingling in my back
then the breaking
to tilt with planetary bodies.

Today I coast ungainly
as a pudgy goose at Como Lake
over the lift off, breathless,
feet dragging on the damasked rug.

Stumblingly
with a shoulder's wrench
down a long gallery
I gaze wistful through glass
practising what I have already forgotten.

Feet Addressing Head

Hey dude, give us some space and grass,
you, rumbling up there
in your bright, abstract buzz.
You could go flying off, incapacitated
without us down here to keep you real,
you in your bulbous, bloodless dome.

Remember, we are your contact with ground zero.
Bathe us with myrrh and balm,
massage us once in a while
and maybe we will remember you
when the two of us lie tip to toe
partnered for the long journey home.

Caliban

My soul longs to flow
into the tattered lace of tides,
but daily constraint,
this hogshead of shelter
confines me in its cube.

I would utter forests.
Something there like God
does not loathe a sigh.

Black Footlocker

I had almost forgotten the black footlocker
belonging to my father during the war

its brass hasps and worn brown leather handle,
the fasteners on either side snapping into place

the musk of its interior, a case for books,
a coffee table, a suitcase for innumerable moves;

how it disappeared one day never to return.
Did I throw it out, take it to the dump,

leave it out in the rain on garbage day?
I ache for its smooth innards,

its resting place for my feet,
the unnecessary weight of it,

covered with stamps as from a journey.

Fistfuls of Dark in the Suburbs

It is a lovely world
in your clean village of honeysuckle trellises,
aerobics centres and pet salons
except for the dehydrated woman
sleeping in a doorway near Hastings and Gore.

It is a winter paradise with delicate icicle lights
strung from the porch
except for the frozen child locked outside
your sliding glass door.

It is lovely and calm in your bunker
except for the fist-bitten dark
and bloodied, stigmatized palms
about to shatter the peace of your aero-dome,
the wild dogs pressing their noses
against your Plexiglas.

It is a small, small, wonderful world after all
except that your head is Siamese-twinned
to the head of a bagman and wet moths
shudder in the lights of your dream.

It is a fine prospect
except for the lean Christs
shadowing your well-exercised flesh
and the starvation whispers of anorexic children.

Writing to Magnolia

When the big sag comes
I say to magnolia,
how satiny your leaves
and add to myself,
it really could be worse
than raking May magnolia petals
into fragrant heaps, delighting
in delicate mauve streaks,
seeing how easily they bruise
how much solitude they require,
how they are shaped like oblong pears.

(She wants what Yeats said woman could never have:
to be loved for herself alone
and not her yellow or auburn hair.)

That and more:
the mastery in love,
and you, Magnolia,
casting your fleshy dress
like snow at my feet.

Dear Prime

You told me your name directly when I found you on our driveway—
Prime, as in *Robin redbreast in his prime*, and *prime,* because you gave
me the gift of your death on the second liturgical hour and because
though you were common, part of the common longing for spring, you
were first and original to me. I held your stillness in my breath, then
moved my fingers into your breast, so recently puffed full blown. You
were warm but your small neck was broken. You must have plunged
into the window of the truck where later I found a few of your casual
feathers, and died with no sound but that one dull thud. I wrapped you
in a towel, brought you to the sink (no flap or flutter), and closed your
enameled eyes, noticing the rust-colour of your breast, burnt orange,
not red at all. Fine feathers bunched back finely along your neck, made
you seem larger than you were, your feet curled away in the stillness
of deep meditation.

Black Owl

I find you on the path,
flaccid mass of feather and bone,
cat ears laid back against your head,
eyes like wild broom, centres of daisies.

Your right wing is dusky as a raven's,
drooped like a broken wishbone,
so I thrust you halfway into my overcoat,
walk the long mile to wildlife refuge
praying all the zigzag way
into your luminous eyes.

The Pause

Hooded owl, horned and snowy owl
of ripened, ringed eyes
grey Arctic wolf in hullabaloo
Canada goose on warmed nest
grub and masticating beetle,
amoeba in wavering dance
subatomic particle in wave's sonata
eight-year-old girl in leggings
pounding a western beach:

let all the earth keep silence

Blessed Are the Poor in Spirit

In some liveable future
I will walk in on my brave
girl self, trying to be perfect.

She is twelve and playing alone in her room
with an early prototype of Barbie
cutting paper dolls with red and blonde
long straight hair, perfect tiny waists.

She is too old for this game
so the room is locked. She is reading
her mother's guide to becoming a woman
and her period has not come; she is behind
all her friends. She has tons of homework
and will turn to it soon
for she wants perfect grades,
so she lies in her bed memorizing
the names and dates under the pictures
though she has a headache and
has just swallowed too many aspirin.

I shall hold her hands and look into her eyes
saying, *There is no Prince Charming.*
You are beautiful without drudgery
and meant to be queenly

but more than doll, consort or queen mother.
Stones and stories are mixing in your blood
and you are sorting them, you are
Rapunzel leaving her tower
to meet herself in the glen.
You are writing yourself and the stories
of women, and poems are bounding out of closets
and file drawers and people care.
You are about something I cannot see.
You are Lady Poverty because you have risked
everything and remained yourself.
You are living off the wages of light
which is feast, and the kingdom
is laid out before your arms, fingers, lips.
What you want is already spread before you
and you do not know it.

A Two-Day Escape from Dullsville

Volunteering to go into a volley
of pre-pubescent hormones
at kids camp where nubile bodies
glow in the dark, small breasts bud

I confiscated all the flashlights,
squawking at the girls till eagles came
in the morning, drowning my voice.
Now I am vanishing into a dot

on the Thetis Island ferry
watching your friends towed
in tubes near the dock, thinking
the zodiac of stars a child of twelve

with some compartments filled,
your hands, mauve starfish gripping down,
your fists, hot pink peony buds
about to admit a world of ants.

For you at twelve, anything is possible,
your taste buds large as a dragon's
at the back of your mouth.
You are balancing sun and moon

like marbles in a whirligig,
becoming a person I never
could have imagined. My love
fiercest in these partings.

Knots

She says she is a worry to herself,
a series of knots, one springing up
just where another was undone,
Gordian, uncuttable,

her agile fingers troubling themselves
all day, sometimes prematurely elated,
then falling back to task—
child labour of the soul.

She is my flesh, my dream,
but her knots have grown full size.
I thank her for the metaphor—
my life too is a tensed cord

at which I pluck and pluck.
What are her dense ligatures?
Homework, exclusions, indifferent boys,
a mind that picks at gravel with the birds?

Who, having survived one adolescence,
would take to it again? Who
can learn from anyone else's rope tricks
those cool sleights of hand?

Among the Elders

Here you stand at twelve
conversing among your elders,
astonishing precocity and power—
breathless parents barely
catching up to see you
slipping across a threshold.

Say, just for the sake of argument,
like that Jewish kid of long ago
you could stand in the full
integrity of your voice,
all the envious adult world poised
for the announcement of some godly business.

Let's say twelve is a breakthrough—
stature, grace, holy scrolls unrolling
from one hand, the other clutching
lip gloss, nail polish, gel,
teen magazines, and angst.
This precipice, you say,
no business of ours.

Heaven Tree

(Carmanah Valley, Vancouver Island)

Fungus climbs your steep side,
lilies cling to the hem of your skirt,
needles extend into the moist air.
Your bole is throne and seat
for many invisible parasites

All feed on you
but you never complain
of their dependency,
being drained, having to sustain
the whole thing in midair

Take, eat—
this is my body
green and brown and unbroken
broken
      for you
           and you

Wilderness/Poetry

The wild deer wandering here and there
Keep the human soul from care.
                        —William Blake, "Auguries of Innocence"

Like all good mothers
she takes time out
in her remote house of cedar.

There is a syllabus we cannot master
            and it has no name.

A burning bush of bright florets.

Once we hiked into an alertness
            of alpine air, showers of quickened lupine
met our gaze, steadily cupping
            and releasing gold pollen
                        too small for touch.

Even when the marmots almost
            played pet for us
begging for biscuits, we knew
            we were a matter of indifference
                        wholly peripheral

and it is good to be dethroned,
          not to be chief priest in the middle
               of the apocalypse
with God the Father above, brutes
          and grass at heel. Here

the abyss is a roiling cauldron
          spewing up forms so lovely
               they silence speech.

We are their metaphor,
          but for what? The presence
has changed before we can name it
          or say, *this,*
               this is the meadow
where we wandered and expelled ourselves
          this earth opening at our feet—

fireweed, paintbrush,
          anemones recklessly imitating old men.

From this, we carved our box hedges
          and English country gardens.

What is the name for a microcosm of ivory
and white explosions contoured by tiny black bugs?

Queen Anne's lace? Not likely.
Unless you can imagine a million

Neoclassical collars
handed out to the populace.

We have argued from deity to design,
but who can conceive a mind this
full of bones and ruminations?

In faith we call it love,
            and move to say how wilderness is poetry
throwing off topiary sonnets,
        driving into *vers libre* to push
                    that order again into a disarray
implying closure
            never closing. Wilderness

breathing solitude
            pauses in its own mirror
                        of glacial ice
                                    cupped by undulating mountains—
            anaphora down a page
chooses the fragile image, lean line of pine along a ridge

intuits and digresses,
            stands witness to itself
                        in bright caesuras

                        where we fall into language

from **A Plot of Light** *(2004)*

Joy

She is Wisdom, my lost child-
self, daughter with sky eyes.

She is Sophia. I am still giving birth
to myself as she gives birth to me

but it doesn't feel painless.
She is Blake's Joy. She is

unplumbed starfire. She is
breathing. Yes. She is.

We are singing to each other
"Happy birthday to you."

The wet child is slipping between
our thighs like a white dolphin.

Star-thrown.

Lacrimae Rerum

The tearfulness of things
has entered my bones.

Why? I cannot recall.
Some heartbreak or other.

Many times since
in times of greater heartbreak

no tears at all. These not-tears
are virgins' lamps,

hot oils anointing starry sky,
cleansing everything.

Nothing remains sullied
in their wake.

Like breakers they soothe
the crisscrossed shore.

Named, Unnamed

First you draw me by my name,
then unname me.

I am under your name as one
nameless.

Yet such tenderness in the calling
of a name.

Anyone so named
can never be completely

lost, having been paid
the utmost attention

as a satin leaf kissed
before leaving the ash

or a beloved dog
before quitting its skin

beside a highway.
Form, skin, essence

all named, loved,
every uncountable

nameless hair
named in the Name—

as trillium under *trefoil*
as Madonna lily under *candor*

as the name falling away
under the name rearing its head.

Pilgrimage

No resting.
The pilgrim hovers over herself

on the steep ascent,
part of her climbing

part still floundering
on the slippery slopes

of the tarns below
in a maze of malls

in a consumer frenzy.
She has left behind her name

but wants some key to reorientation.
The orient man in saffron

has implicated her
in an intricate plot of light.

Coming up to a halfway house
neither here nor there

she pleads for directives.
If you really desire the kingdom come,

he says, *love this dark sod;*
then kisses ground zero

where wild goldenrod nod
in a cloud of lit mist.

Love Your Enemies

What if the dreamer surrendered herself
to the scary man in the bear costume?

The children might escape,
leaving the man beating his fists on the ground.

What kind of evil does he portend?
Rape? Murder? Systemic violence?

He is not a person or a country.
His dance of hatred and rage

strips and steals the skins of animals
to disguise a bottomless fear.

Of what is he afraid?
Children's spontaneous laughter,

toothless gums at the breast,
a future that does not know his name?

Perhaps his own emptiness, if he halts the offence.
The dreamer stands stock still on shore

imagining both her certain extermination
and the strange thing love might do

to change the weary, inarticulate
bulk of him, or loosen the knots of his heart

should she take him in her arms.

The Prayers of the Animals

The notion of some infinitely gentle/ Infinitely suffering thing.
                                    —T.S. Eliot, "Preludes"

The kin-dom of heaven is a lens
to wide-open turquoise eyes

sea-quarried saucers of the black
and white lions who are unselfish.

The purest and most beautiful
is hard driven over a cliff.

His bones are broken again;
flanks flayed in everyone.

The mushroom cloud is not a prediction
but the fear from which we hide our faces.

Truth is, such lions cannot be killed.
Let's suppose many small animal helpers

real animals of many species and tribes,
breathe the breath of life

into the wounded heap that is the lion's bones.
Suppose for an instant

we are indebted to the prayer of Fox
with his bushy tail on red alert,

or Mink, with her winsome peering,
and that even the warrior Hawks

whose pitiless minds,
are caught off-guard (for a moment)

by some *infinitely gentle,*
infinitely suffering thing

resounding in their hearts,
splintering the Armageddon cloud.

Dream Cables

for my spiritual mentor Olga Park, 1891-1985

Who tore down the cables
so none of mine got through?

How could I forget her living voice?
She taught me to play chords

as a master pianist presses
hands over a student's on the keys.

And the squeaky discord
she called music.

In the humility of beginnings,
she assumed proficiency would come,

showing, "letting go into silence"—
the boomerang of grace,

Divinity in the dimmed violet,
Goddess in the sunflower.

All the rooms that spill from her house
as the cottage rebuilds itself

through cords and pinions of prayer
are warmed by her syllables sounding the air.

On Contemplation, at a Merton Conference

Better not to define it.
Every moment brings new seeds.

Call it a long loving look at the real,
an eremitic gaze at Mt Canigou.

Symposium of seekers,
wayfarers gathered.

A Presence that dismisses nothing,
rounding tired selves in its arms,

lounges comfortably on the back step
of the conference room.

Poetry dwells too in generous dark
awaiting the one

who will press into her forehead
a fine blue flame.

"The Faces of Living Things Are All Alike"

—Black Elk

The elegant French lady's face, carved reredos,
the German teen's face, sadly efficient,
the English, American, Canadian faces
more like my own, sharing a common tongue,
the Spanish taxi driver's face, ivory against a dark cloud,
the amiable faces of the street dogs in Prades,
the swirled faces of scarlet poppies alongside a road,
the wide, arresting face of the albino gorilla in the Barcelona zoo,
the cautious faces of two Muslim men
sporting American flag t-shirts in the airport lounge,
the pursed face of the uneasy millionaire,
the bland face of the street snail
poking up out of its intricate staircase of shell.

Faces of stars in a kingdom's blind corner

In My Mother's House Are Many Mansions

In my Mother's house
        (drinking blackcurrent tea with lemon)
I am a work-in-progress
        (folding back pages and scribing marginalia)
having an into-the-body experience
        (by peach brick walls)
from ex-stasis to in-stasis
        (soft as flesh)
climbing from the womb on a ladder of bones
        (grammar of laughter)
What embedded worry-cross
        (right in the middle of her forehead)
uncrosses itself on the first night
        (even though she was horrid)
Brown moth by the poolside
        (folding back lanced wings)
completes its karma and dies
        (object of silken attention).
A deer has walked the labyrinth before me
        (dear deer)
Remembering the goddesses in the tale
        (sharing one eye among them)
she is glad for her one eye
        (watching it pass from hand to hand).

Migrating into God

Time to lose the habitual motions—
from the flicking of the switch
to the thoughtless word.

Time to do a stint at release,
to unclasp clasping
as when peridot beads

slide from the neck
and white arms fall
from the prison of their hold.

Time to set the heart afloat
in the wide grey strait
with the wild island geese.

Building the Spiritual Body

Not like a leaky apartment, board by board,
but more like a secret doorway of the brain,
as when Kepler first imagined Neptune
burning in its gaseous haze.

So what was always present
floats at last into our domain,
like the vagrant planets
with their blue and orange moons,
red spots on Jupiter
brewing a continual storm.

Tender Inward

You save me from the temptation to fly
from metaphor into dry abstraction
connecting me to spiralling songbird's cry
that pierces heaven, nuances every action.
I kiss the tender inward of your hand,
a daybed where skittering shadows dream
your kindness, the abundance of the land,
eagles' consortium by a salmon stream.
To say I know you is true and untrue,
your thoughts and habits, sensible and clear;
yet part of you, while I was sleeping, grew
to boundless amplitudes inside the ear
where the Lover in secret uncovers
oiled hinges, then opens doors to lovers.

Falling

(in memory of my father, Donald Arthur McCaslin, 1921-1987)

The falling begins at work.
I get a call that you have gone over
without warning like a giant cedar,
crashing across filing cabinets,
gashing your lip, head.

At home you topple
on the way back from the mailbox,
shatter your hip
just as my husband and I leave for Europe.
I phone from Dublin and your voice
tries to sound normal, cheering.

The doctors don't know why
these fits of un-coordination,
muscles listless, unresponsive,
finally announcing Lou Gehrig's disease,
the same that quelled your uncle Don.

Over the phone again
you call this your "death sentence."

I am steeped in black ice—
the finality of words.

Progeny

Eight years into my marriage
when you are dying, and have given up
on a grandchild through me
(my brother has given you two),
I carry one-month old Claire Iris
to the room where you are lying
helpless, tended by my brother,
the one who stayed home.

It has always been as if you believed
you would survive only through your progeny,
the purpose of life being to reproduce.

Mom had only wanted two,
but you would have had twelve
like the old patriarchs.

Once when she refused to have a third,
little "Carl," you said, "who would never be,"
she caught you cutting holes in a condom.

Now, through you, I am faced with Job's conundrum,
why good people suffer, why accident, why disease?

Yet a month after Claire dances into time
I lay her on your chest—belated offering—
new life palliating brokenly against your departing.

Dream

Before you die you tell me a dream
of how you found yourself
hurtling across space to the other side
of the universe, fearless, exhilarated,
as if on an exploratory flight.

I feel this is not a mere beating
of the chemistry of the brain
against nullity.

To me it seems no individuality
so complex can lapse,
relapse into nothing.

What pavilions did you build here
that rose to meet you there?
To what did your dark night open?

Elegy

My daughter came, my father went away
within the circle of a single year—
one joy, one grief, held in two seasons' sway.

The biting loss not tempered, held at bay.
When death's the summit, who can conquer fear?
When daughter came, my father went away.

For everyone who toils, one comes to play.
Upon the viper's nest, the innocent's tear.
One joy, one grief held in two seasons' sway.

I bind my grief in rhyme to make it fray
like perishable cloth unravels and is sear
till daughter comes, and father's gone away.

This death, this life, merge in a single way
by which we come and go and learn to bear
one joy, one grief held in two seasons' sway.

From one bright light rebounds a two-fold ray.
My daughter, come, my father, pass away—
one joy, one grief held in two seasons' sway.

from **Lifting the Stone** (2007)

Cleave a piece of wood,
I am there;
lift up the stone
and you will find me there.

—from The Gospel of Thomas

Heresies

Here is the heresy of the mind
rising above the body as if
the two had never been lovers

as if there were no telltale musk,
no confluence of rivers, no
intertwining of hairs long and short.

Here is the heresy of the body
abandoning memory, excommunicant,
silenced down the stairstep spine.

But here too, somehow, the healing
communion of saints, the skin
a clear mirage, the body almost drinkable.

Here is the resurrection of the dead
in reservoirs of hearing,
aspens quaking in a wind's sarabande.

Here is the life everlasting—
generations gathered together
like sweet plums in a bowl.

Psyche

Obscure and rare that state to which I fell
or rose, no, floated awake into your invisible arms.

You whispered, *Désirée*, and touched me with a thousand
exquisite fingers—a rush like hummingbird wings

filtering through every parcel from crown to toe to crown,
crescendoing, falling, continuing night's extravagant enterprise

when we flowed and spiralled in the chakras of the spine,
blossomed in the thousand-petalled lotus of the brain.

You were not in and out and away like any ordinary lover,
but lingered all night, sequestering, calling me *Beloved*.

A Dream of Thomas Merton

How is it the monk (un-habited) is not surprised,
sitting cross-legged on a patch of earth
trading jokes and cold beer?

Talk of Martin Luther King, Osama, fallen towers,
nothing new under the sun

(except his arch eyes, a high-energy discharge).

"Jesus was the kind of doctor
who would heal anyone who asked—
criminal, insane. No flinching or thinking of bounds."

He pronounces his own new name,
"Threshold Dweller"—
one who hops like Raven across portals.

Waking, I think how straightaway
I felt his mettle, knowing
he had been fed fire—

                        I, grain

Preceptor

Bulletins tumbled from evanescence.
She knew and did not know who she was.

You have not remembered me, as is fitting,
except as her dazed interlocutor

her scanty peephole on the world.
My presumptuous critiquing of her poems

became my purgatory, now purged.
Even her epistles were nothing

but metaphor, cochineal under drab.
This quickened nobody wouldn't sign

but in pale strokes of pencil on a card,
as if to efface her name. Thankfully,

she did not absorb one whit of my advice:
"Get rid of the dashes—regularize the grammar."

Intensity played hide-and-seek with time,
genius volcanic in the interstices.

I was blind. I let her sign, "Your scholar,"
then, to my abiding glory, "Friend."

Had I died in the uncivil trenches of the South,
"Higginson" would be moribund.

Yet I survive in her wild—a man
who held, briefly galactic in his palm,

revolving *resonance of emerald,*
hummingbird in muslin's white.

Omega Suite

The greatest taboo is spirituality.
                    —Carl Jung

Light like cracked glass and the Christ-Sophia
with a bucket of stars falling in our ears.

The best thing on record, The kin-dom of heaven
is within you.

It is not divine anger undressing before you,
but your own enmity against the earth.

I carry a small, white stone in my pocket,
and every time I rub it there's a prayer for you.

Whatever they force on you won't be the thing—
whatever you find for yourself will be.

The poet enters the particulars,
already a plenum,
antennae up, attending the flow.

Arachnids

levitate through their brief burgeoning,
                silkily cast

armoured, lofted
                Knights Templar, ladies bountiful

acrobats slung in silent safety nets
                dancing high wires of verse

        skittering on a tensile of their own making.

Chickadee

Black-capped chickadee
        (fleshed messenger and message)
startles an inner dullness.

Trill summons my meditation,
lifts it
over the steering wheel and beyond the car.

Small feet braced
eyes flecked
with quick intent.

Dear bird,
return and draw again
        that keening song,
        that circling kaddish on loan to air.

Dog

Crouched at our camps,
sleeping in our caves

tethered, corded, leashed
companion in the hunt.

If we bow and bow,
we cannot atone

for the dodge, the cringe.
Your romp and drool

fully moment-wise,
teach us to relish loam—

you, Nose of Creation,
rolling tumult in grass

vocabulary unencompassed
by "come," "sit," "stay."

Kindred Kine

Two lopsided cows
knuckle-kneed
flick droning flies,
lick each other's
wind-weathered sides,
capsizing at dusk
under the hill.

Two heads lift
as a woman passes.

Grooming resumes,
joint leanings
each into each,
a shelter of tongues.

Who is to say these companions
inclining toward dark
do not move those soft tongues
against the day of their slaughter?

Moth

On a white ledge
        arrayed in a beige silk shift

your wings
        (strophe and antistrophe)
                inside the morning light.

How you evaded webs, lightbulbs, brooms,
        laid yourself out
                in stippled breaths

surrendered
        to this flowing light
                travelling from the one to the one

so now
        all that matters is
                the colour of the soul.

Lifting the Stone

Lift up the stone, and you will find me there.
                    —The Gospel of Thomas

Suddenly from the very pivot
of wrenching horror—forgiveness,

a shift, a loosening.
One death enters the only world.

Suddenly
past talk of atonement and sin

one dies in this very death
I carry in my arms.

Suddenly it is clear
what must be done
                    and why the voice says,

          Do nothing.

Not quietism this,
for in the dust
          motes dance.

She has been under the rocks
and in the hard places of dreams

to record the most peripheral arabesques.

Besotted with Jesus

Still besotted with Jesus after all these years
despite the unfashionableness of such love
unconscionable history of the Church
sad path of pillage, persecution, crusade
racism, war and rumours of war.

Despite heart horrors held in continuance
　　　　　some record and reverberation extends
　　　　　　　　　shimmering to the enemy (ourselves).

What a Mediterranean peasant began
remains untried
except in the shock and awe of saints

those human frailties, marginal men and women
　　　　　(Francis, Teresa, Gandhi, Mandela, Weil)

stunning the warrior Hate
　　　　　　　　　(healers, transformers).

Call me Christian Jew Buddhist Hindu Sufi
　　　　　(whatever you like)

big fruit salad of the Spirit
    every flavour savoured

        drenched in a common juice
        culled in unnameable mind

      (Krishna, Wakan Tanka, Gaia, Dionysius, Sophia)
      Peerless Peer

all and none of the above.

Shame

1

Each day the music
whether we will or no.

Outside, magnolia's unfurling
slims the air

even now uniting the worlds we are,
one divided current,

heads devouring hearts, heads
marching backwards as to war:

"Hallelujah, glory, *gory,* hallelujah."
"Holy holy holy," saith the wind.

Shame falls out of the sky.
Crash helmets, gas masks, tanks,

hungry voices of children in the loaded air.
Who will heal the frightened enemy—"ourself?"

Stock market graphs—barometers of greed.
"Shock and awe" of terror's inhuman blast

unveils no weapons of mass destruction
but our own.

2

Across from the Langley Colossus,
tranced faces munch burgers
while Baghdad blazes
on screens one and two,
the hockey game on screen three.

Thank God it's finally Friday
and off to the movies for something
vicariously violent or
maybe a "chick flick"
to distract from the horror that is
our daily bread.

3

Here on the lawn, Magnolia, lover, beloved,
shudders to her roots

knowing April will swell in her again,
releasing love's ample white blossoms

once more into the unreceiving atmosphere.

Radiant Body

*For as the soul is a being of the cosmic order, it is
absolutely necessary that it should have an estate
or portion of the cosmos in which to keep house.*

—Philoponus

Perhaps heaven shelters in this elbow
resting on this desk, where hand cradles chin,
or out there in Orion thoughts intend
to lean into this place and grow
lungs, or go four-footed, or on wings,
so says the circulating word that sings

news from nowhere, mystery in the wheels,
surprise—whatever awakened Ezekiel
who though broken, half in hell
considered no negotiations, no deals.
If all of me belongs in several worlds,
when body ages and leaf-like curls

it is possible some radiant skin
will flare within this flesh,
a denser light, forgotten guest,
arise familiar like lost kin.
What if earth houses more than we know—
some subtle-bodied dream of long ago?

In a Room Called Resurrection

A young and a middle-aged woman
are cupped in sleep.

In a room called waking
walls open to corridors,

give way to antechambers
and quiet terrariums

solariums where tent caterpillars
meander up and down

through tender shoots, choosing
the most ordinary leaves

softly denting the foliage
with small persistent mouths.

Monarch butterflies weave
slow paths in air, and above

drops of sun swirl
and walls collapse

slung octaves of flowerbeds
like hidden stairs spiralling.

Seven Ways of Looking at the Kin-dom Prayer

1
Ubiquitous Presence,

let your realm descend
(ours being so small).

Your will be done
(ours, too limited).

Help us locate our will
within yours

till earth is perceived
as it is, heaven,

where all things are unified
beyond our separatist notions.

Let us dance in the grand hullabaloo,
not muting the music.

Give us this day what we most need,
knowing everything flows from you,

and walk with us steadily to
the great self-emptying.

Be close when mortmain calls,
you, our deepest interiority,

dancing still on the green.

2
Burning One,
you, flaming in earth and in heaven,

holy in luminosity,
holy in darkness.

Let your presence so blaze
that there is no more difference

between your kin-dom
and the kin-doms of this world.

Let us feed the hungry
till no one is malnourished,

and help us circulate
more constantly in the deep forgiving.

Keep us from self-alienation
which hides our original faces from us.

Ache in us for justice
till you set up a tent in our hearts

forever.

3
Dearest Helper,
Author, Muse, Matrix,

we are your far-flung flotsam,
fortuitous night-seed,

stanza without end—
time's branching poem.

Amen.

4
For parents who wounded unknowingly—
a child's forgiveness.

For those not yet healed of childhood trauma—
self-love.

For the closed fist—
grace.

For those desiring a sterile outward order rather than
the fecund tumble of chaos—fearlessness.
For the riot of names that is God's unnameable body—
vision.

For a sweep of sand carved by an aqua sea—
awe.

5
Holy One,
expand our cramped encampments.

Lower your world so imperceptibly into ours,
the two become one in our perceiving.

Help us to take only what we need
and embrace us in the endless conjoining.

Open our hearts in the turmoil
and keep us permeable to your spirit.

6
Welcome, Holy Presence,
You who unite heaven and earth.

Feed us, your fledglings, release us
into the cornucopia air

where there is no "mine" and "yours."
Break upon us

when we slip on the stair.

Propel our propositions
like scrolls into the sea.

Rescue us from opinion.
Transmute our desire

and make us again, beginners.

7
Our Mater,

holy in matter,
matter in us again.
You, sea spray and firework,
calm keeper of geological ages,

dignify our cells.
Place us once more among the order of wild things.

Water Corona

1

To meditate on water in her many transformations—
runnel's zest, creek's crouch, waterfall's
leap, glacier's gathered tears,
the promises of wells—
is a privilege of the hydrated,
but those whose cells pant
for water's deepest ministry
cry for a dram to parched throats,
flow that embraces the human
and more than human worlds.
So, it is our luck to contemplate
the pure springs of dreams,
to wake, thirsting, fill a glass brim-full,
enjoy what is not limitless balm.

2

What is not limitless balm arose
from a limitless source, dense heart
bursting from the original fireball.
How is it a galaxy of fiery arms
nourished such bonding? Who married
your molecules in a streaming bed
and sang their epithalamion to the stars?

Gaia, dressed in dripping firmaments,
announced your arrival, wrapped you
in a receiving blanket of blue silk.
Islands floated on your primordial
stream, whose depths bred starfish,
butterfly fish, crab, coral, sea anemone,
a turbulence from which we might not have emerged.

3

A turbulence from which we might not have emerged
became your journeywork; cells said your name
and we swam forth, abandoning our fishy tails.
Your pulse in the amniotic caves
was a canyon-carving softness.
Soon sky reflected your greys and greens.
When you enacted your birth in our bodies,
you graced us with mineral springs,
underground streams, secret grottos
for our ablutions and ceremonies,
lifting us up and dipping us down
in the rivers of your voice,
Mother, matrix—licking the newborn
with your large wet tongue.

4

With your large wet tongue,
you gentle us, tend us as we drop

from your side, cooling our foreheads.
Soon we climb, bearing our sweat and gear
up the peak to find you stretched
solitary between mountains, startling
our possibilities with glacial blue.
Despoilers of such wild reserve—
contenders, dumpers, extractors
from a mechanistic school—build dams
over and against your living body,
pronounce you "other," marked for our use.
Eagle, with knife-edge skill, plummets deep,
feeds in your empire, while we drown in our own.

5

Feeding in your empire, while we drown in our own,
the animals enter the slow crucifixions of water.
Children retreat from shore, deer shrink
from creeks. Fertilizers, pesticides, plastics,
car emissions infect your pores,
the water cycle breaks on its wheel,
condensation falls as acid rain
on the keening heads of whales.
Valleys flood and dry at human command.
Underground springs, your last refugees,
fugitive, crouching in your dark,
sense computers plotting
the extraction of your marrow—
though one living drop could save the world.

6

Though one living drop could save the world,
we stop our ears to your music.
Water ascends angelic
in the stems of roses, descends
over cliffs in self-abandonment.
Nothing is more humble than water,
brother, sister, seeking the lowest place,
washer of feet, and of our souls,
those reservoirs, containing us,
shaping our bodies' fluid estate.
Though we boil in cauldrons,
hibernate in cisterns, sink stiff-necked in ice,
your forms continue melting
snow's white compact around the heart.

7

Snow's white compact around the heart
numbs, and private greed for public
gift may extinguish our species.
"Let justice flow like water," says the prophet.
When polar ice caps melt, climates climax,
and floods ransack the world,
who will choose—now—this day—
to bend to water's ways?
Becoming tributaries to water, we
might serve what eye cannot fathom,

mysterious in her mingling with earth,
air, fire—Thales' Elemental Queen,
hydrosphere hymned in this meditation
on water in her myriad transformations.

from **Demeter Goes Skydiving** *(2011)*

The mysteries remain,
I keep the same
cycle of seed-time
and of sun and rain;
Demeter in the grass
I multiply,
renew and bless…

—H.D., from *Red Roses for Bronze*

Demeter Goes Skydiving

to get an aerial view of the sucking terrain
where the ground gaped and devoured her daughter.
She glimpses the iron-walled, underground mall,
its gates, trendy shops, thinning hype,
the Armani machismo of its Overlord,
politico, numb, sprawled in his corporate death.

Arms akimbo, she freefalls, wearing out gravity,
head over splayed feet tumbling absurdly through space,
plummeting, eyes half-closed, wincing almost
as she awaits the jerk of the tightening cords,
the chute that will or will not catch her.

She could call on Cupid or a sylph, no doubt,
but doesn't, though wind tears her cornsilk hair.
Crazy kamikaze void of music; her body,
unstately skywriting limned on Zeus's vault,
as if anything mattered after the wasting of her child.

She spells across the heavens, "Womb ache."
A slam poem slaps into the ground that is herself, Enna,
while her lost one puzzles over the seeds of a pomegranate,
all that she will allow herself in the bed of the dark king

who likes his women lean in their brief resistance.

Hades' Gym

When he tires of dispensing pharmaceuticals
(Effexor/ elixir, Paxil/ peace pill,
Prozac/ musack, Celexa for Alexa),

he self-medicates by hanging out at his gym
over the door of which posters blare:
"Don't Wait for the Grim Reaper."

"Run Yourself Into the Ground Now."
"Control is Pleasure."
"Addiction, the Happy Affliction."

Teens and pensioners pound their heels
on the fluorescent-lit treadmills of the dank underground,
trying to work up a sweat under posters of Sisyphus.

"I must, I must, develop my bust"
shoots from the mouths of anorexic grandmas,
a sad plainsong, all the poetry they know

in the land of the depressing dumps,
the glut of naught
and poppy seed croissants.

Persephone, with a bump in her tummy,
does lunges, counts off a hundred sit ups on the ball,
stares into the mirror on the wall.

Multi-tasking is a breeze.
Read about all the subterranean stars
(who's fat, who's thin, who's out, who's in).

"While pounding the stairmaster, nothing's a disaster."

The hungry ones outside the gate,
the bombed-on shrieking children blown sky high,

can all be muffled for the buff at heart.

Persephone in Hades

Awake as one dead among the dead,
I hear voices whisper I look pale
and inquire if I've been ill.

Some do not see me at all.
Some shudder and turn.
The snow is a crust I cannot consume.

I walk in my own tracks
past curbside detritus—
melancholic meanderings.

There is no regret,
though neighbours stare
at the nameless wraith,

and thrust in my hair
their querulous glances.
Yet I to myself am solid

as dice thrown by the wayside.
Feet like roots walking,
a churning aimlessness.

Only Cerberus, curious, sniffs my fingers.

Persephone Tours the Underground

on Hermes' electric golf cart,
zooms through dropping corridors,
past flinching factories, stifling cells
where skeletal children sew
designer emblems day and night
on the jeans of privileged teens,

witnessing how the upper world
rests on the muscle of billions below,
how the cosmos has become a pyramid scheme,
not the circular dream of Eleusis,
how, here, even fireflies shed their luminescence
and no light blesses tortured, bloodied heads,

how the somnolent stumble on zigzag trails,
lugging poisoned water in pails,
how to reign as Hades' Queen is to lurch
with the uncountable destitute
under ignorant, affluent feet, (the uneasy gambit
of those above who have seen, considered
and turned away).

Persephone Hears a Layered Singing

Flanked by milling shoppers
jockeying for positions in line-ups,
I walk through a labyrinthine, underground mall,
past elegant makeup counters, robotic joggers,
into rooms of stockpiled merchandise,
oil tanks, missiles, endless silent hallways

that open at last on a corn-yellow room
where light streams from a skylight
on the braided head of a woman
playing a grand piano and singing.

She is not young or old, familiar or unfamiliar,
but has the timbre of one who had been my mother,
one long thought dead.

And what a voice, as of all octaves slung together,
an Ella voice, a rich contralto hymning "Summertime,"
voice broken and repaired in each measure,
voice beyond control and controlling
voice of longing and release
voice of resisting and yielding,
voice making no division
between upper and lower worlds,

liminal, liberating voice without score
no ulterior motive but to sing
the song which is the world
in all its rich atonalities, lifts, and falls.

(For if one can so sing, anything may be possible.)

So this is how I come to the upper world,
not shoving one foot before the other,
but remaining where I am and rising on a voice.

Often now, I am in the deep underground
and simultaneously above,
being both spring and winter,
all seasons rotating together.

Demeter Pauses at the Foot of the Kokanee Glacier

So far west, past prairies
into avalanche fields that swallow children whole

into thrusting breaths of purest air
where for a nanosecond sorrow lifts

like cloud cover, unveiling acres of rock
where even old Thunderfinger cannot penetrate,

deep into the ground of an interior weeping
that makes the bluest blue of lakes.

Here, the wide-eyed, deep-girt anemone flaunts,
fireweed flames past fear of being plucked.

This time the goddess does not compromise
but surrenders her fertility to snowfields

singing, I am She,
Isis gathering dismemberment in her arms,

Mary weeping at the foot of the cross,
all wandering, grieving mothers

brought to prescience in my body.
I am She, sleeves of silver flashing over the Slocan.

Part of my daughter is beside me now
and part of her is out of reach

though nothing is unto itself enough
in these alpine floral sprays.

Demeter Laughs

I, Ianthe, old serving woman,
claim honour from the gods
for making the post-menopausal Demeter guffaw.

With one risqué joke, a bit of raillery,
she who had been silent, veiled,
refusing to quaff my herbal brew,
suddenly felt the mirth rising from her left side,
a swelling from the basement of the belly,
staccatoed through the chambers of the chest.

First a giggle, then a titter,
passed from gut to brain
to heart, to lung, to eye to feet,
a cavorting roundelay
converting the whole household
to taboo-breaking rebirth.

Laughter sang in her
(definitely post-hormonal)
through double dark

till she fell off her stool,
and all the long-gripped fury
leaked through the interstices of the room

and she, a goddess in hiding,
could not cup the explosion
or in any way contain it.

Demeter Tries to Adopt Britney Spears

Britney, America's erstwhile darling
at twelve, now fodder for YouTube,
her half-life held in Pepsi ads.

Cornered by paparazzi, she swings
her bared bum out of cars
too late to avoid the crotch shot.

"Hit me baby one more time"
with your cameras
en route to the custody trial,
coon-ringed eyes veering away.

Too soon modified, mortified,
commodified, too soon married,
lean, a fatty chomped by the machine,
you, no heavier than Venus in her prime,
you, of the infatuating perfumes
no one will buy.

They have ripped you apart like Orpheus
and your stripped fragments fly all over the web
where your shaven head still goes on singing.

So I'm swooping in for an aerial pickup,
nabbing you by taxi,
smuggling you out of rehab
for Paris, with or without the kids,
where we'll dance on Marc Chagall's ceilings
and I'll introduce you to his mystic bride,
the fiercely flying animals

and you can lie on the beach with Reubens,
where the fans who gobbled you up like candy
can never mock you again
and you will be calmed,
if not wholly convinced,
of your hidden wholeness.

Gaia

When she first rolled out of herself
there was nothing,
just infinite folds of her own
humid flesh, diorama of a volcanic brain.

She attended an inner quickening,
pulse upstaging any Blitzkrieg
humans could devise, humans,
those delirious, unpredictable ones

she would name "natals"—"born of woman."

Their impending chatter was nothing
to her uninterrupted eruptions,
firework festivals.

So she dandled Tyrannosaurus
on mountainous knees,
set him on a plain—
mere smoothing of her lap.

Then formed a crust sprouting
scarlet-scented leaves,
crocuses weeping dew.

They say Uranos, Starry Sky,
covered her in the thunder
of new roilings between them

but, in truth, she covered him
as he went under and down.

And though, in their first orgasm,
she saw the trenches, rapine, landmines,
sutures sewn millennia later in her ageless flesh,

she continued bearing children, undaunted
by all their armaments and Armageddons.

Old Love

Burning even yet,
the ancient one weeps into the fissures,
tracks and trestles of the brain,
lightened by gardenia's fragrant phrase,
older even than coupling earth and sky,
hatched question without amen—
such a dogged gentleness.
How old, old love,
from what abyss cast up?
The old in each other's arms,
mother dancing her calf,
tensile wing of eldest Eros,
dark in the mediate zone,
a voice like shale,
birthing a nautilus child,
slung in the slender femur
and breastbone of salvation.
The days of the avatars have passed,
for we are avatars all,
our small flames quickening.

Our small, quickening flames
when we shall all be avatars
and the days of the avatars have passed.
There is a breastbone of salvation,
life slung in the slender femur,
where nautilus child births
with a voice like shale,
dark in the mediate zone
tensile wing of eldest Eros,
who dances her calf.
The old in each other's arms,
from the abyss cast up
from old, old Love,
a dogged gentleness,
hatched question without amen,
older than coupling earth and sky
lightened by gardenia's fragrant phrase,
tracks and trestles of the brain,
the ancient one weeping into fissures,
burning even yet.

How to Love an Old Dog without Anthropomorphism or Sentimentality

Probably impossible.

But when you take him strolling,
let him linger at trees, posts, hydrants.

Don't jerk his head with the leash,
for he needs to absorb a world beyond your gaze.

Even with cataracts and ear fungus,
his senses are still a thousand times

more world-caressing than yours,
his adoration of the earth more earthy,

more enamoured of grittiness and scent.

Remember how has a pup he tugged
and you could not keep his pace?

Now you jerk him away
from his slow digestion of the real.

Though he surpasses you in dog-years,
he has not tasted death

but worshipped all his life
at the shrine of the Mother.

Don't confuse anthropomorphizing
with conceding to him his passions.

Remember Descartes,
who insisted beasts knew no pain

though they howled on science's wrack.
Honour Pavlov's dogs

whose tests proved (as if we did not know it before),
how easily we can make mechanisms of ourselves.

The Gospel of Mary Magdalene

You are the light you have been moving towards,
said Mary, a woman of intimacies,
who spoke in silence an interior speaking,
high to low, in to out, leaf to branch.

Said Miriam, a woman of intimacies,
cored, yoked, interwoven with matter,
low to high, out to in, branch to leaf:
There is no sin in the waking world.

for we are cored, yoked, interwoven with matter,
yet all that is composed shall be decomposed;
there is no sin in the waking world;
a babe strung in a hammock shoots into the night sky.

Yet all that is composed shall be decomposed.
So Peter and Andrew repudiated the woman's words,
while a babe in a hammock shot into the night sky
and emptied herself as from a tomb.

Peter and Andrew repudiated the woman's words,
whose hair swept by anointing stars,
who emptied herself as from a tomb
becoming awe and the fully human

whose hair swept by anointing stars,
who spoke in silence, an interior speaking,
becoming awe and the fully human:
You are the light you have been moving towards.

Together, We Are Rain

(a Vancouver poem)

Rain I, you, we, it, she, us: rain rhymes rhythmic, arrhythmic,
  precipitous rushing.

Aquatically-challenged cousin Fred said if we moved to the wet coast
  we would
acclimatize to such alluvial aquatics, and like ducks, grow moss on
  our backs.

It was so. Soon submerged in soggy, sumptuous rainforest drizzle,
interior arteries become aqueducts for rainfalls of green frogs.
It was us. We were rain and rain was us. We poured ourselves out
  and spilled over.

Not that this was unpleasant. We adapted, noting that being porous
  and permeable,
notwithstanding drenching, has definite advantages. One can seep
  into a lover, fall
near like dew, transform from dew to ice, then on a whim, nodding,
navigate rivers of bright sun and become a curtain of golden rain.
Numinous, our circular cycle from cumulus, to deluge, to rising
  mist is us.

Runnels and rivulets of us seek together some common source.
Rain invents in dialogue with sun the multiple names of green.
Rain reigns in Cascadia; let Montana weep if it can.
Rain in this bioregion grows cleansing tears.
Rain splashes on whales' heads and the roots of thirsty hydrangeas.
Rain ripples and runs like a renegade while California covets our
    water.
Rain pauses for breath, and the sun, valued tenfold, dances.
Rainmakers, rain dancers in Arizona dream of us as heaven.

Earth As It Is

As above, so below.
But it is not so, no.

Instead the muck-brown river,
sacked vault of heaven

and ourselves vandals
razing ancestral groves

the great alcove
imagined out there

beyond lunar satellites
interstellar voids

rather than within
ourselves, thought's other side,

an opening, maybe here
beneath fermenting blackberries

touchable delectation,
heaven still stabled, lodged, as it is.

from **The Disarmed Heart** *(2014)*

I choose the term "Peace" for that Harmony of Harmonies which calms destructive turbulence and completes civilization. Thus a society is to be termed civilized whose members participate in the five qualities—Truth, Beauty, Adventure, Art, Peace.

—Alfred North Whitehead, *Adventures of Ideas*

O Banana Slug

How you mimic the yellow and brown
alder leaves cast on our driveway
You, hermaphrodite, with eyestalks
poking the moist air

Your crosswise pace carries
the metaphor of your length
from here to where you want to go
six or more inches a minute

more surely than my jumping thoughts
that begin in the body
but land in disaster zones
creating fancies of future loss

(myself shipwrecked in a wheelchair or worse)

while you, faithful to your job
recycle leaves and detritus
decomposing, composting
a softer music stretched across time

Handless, you transit in a slow-swift crawl—
            oarless barge

While I head off for blood work, more tests,
you keep moving, everything working perfectly
in a nervous system simpler, less warlike
than mine, but adequate for all your needs

O Crow

pirouetting on a streetlamp
your instrument

for Cirque du Soleil manoeuvres,
casting your flecked eye streetward

pitching us street slang, noir song
we interpret as a "caw" or "cackle"

actually less a grate or rasp
than a finessed blast:

What I do is me: for that I came

Such a solitary iamb
ta-dumming against cumulus

Dangerous calligrapher
Don Juan Castaneda hipster—

Pitch Black zero—
Dark Night of the Stroll

Where away?

O Black Cottonwood

(Glen Valley, Langley, British Columbia)

I stood still and was a tree amid the wood.
—Ezra Pound

Your saffron leaves unselve us
hollowed trunk a doorway
summoned from forest floor

Melded branches winding
whispered texts entangled
torqued to speechless autumn skies

flaming torsos rising
mottled leaves dropping
honed to shape of tears

What would take you out
hang for sale signs by the roadway
all in the name of development

de-creating where children
breathe in the moist greening
courtship cries of wild barred owls?

O Lovers' Tree

I fell in love with a forest
and became an activist

but first there was you
one, no, two, two cedars twinned

around the heartwood of a tree husk
a realm—two torsos attuned

stretched limb to limb
two root systems' wet entangling

two of you ascending
splitting, reuniting

like Plato's round being
against the gods of progress

against those who would chainsaw
your wide open hearts

And, yes, you pant toward union
under the sky canopy

bride-ing the soar of day
palm to palm like holy palmers' kiss

blessed jointure each to each
pressed each into the other's ahhhh

So, silenced at your lichened knees
I surrender all

to the forest which makes
and remakes your lust and breath

your aching stately pavane

O Christ Cedar

You among emerald drapery
from your wind-
stormed outpost

plank and plane
vertical-horizontal world pivot
sprung from coastal seed

humming core
flaking bark
woodpecker's grail

growing a wilder carpentry
taller masonry
more commodious poem

Be in us the world's resinous heart
hung in a speckled sky—
forest green

hoist and balance
equipoise and reach
sylvan singer   song

O Han Shan

Zesty poet-monk
timewarps from China
to rural B.C.

Action-rouser
hangs hermit thoughts
on Western Red Cedar

Planet's big climate-shapers
(Fir, Black Cottonwood)
spray spritzers in our mouths

Old Han Shan
(more spritely than a teen)
drops rime on twigs

Words rare
as Pacific Water Shrew
ascend a mushroom stair

Leaves' trills dangle
verbs. Ephemeral elaborations
scrawled on deep-time rocks

Hiroshima and Nagasaki Explained

When I was twelve my father explained
how Americans had to drop atomic bombs
on Hiroshima and Nagasaki
"to save all those American lives"

Some inner explosion then
began turning the world ashen
some weight added itself to the heart
that the heart itself could not measure

Something pushed like a mushroom cloud
into my adulthood, printing ghosts
on white walls, horror in the shadows
of a child's burnt hand

Dank Tureen

(a dream about global warming)

Swimming the Australian crawl in a dank tureen,
the sides' sleek stainless steel without traction or edge

Treading water, slowly treading in a heavy dark
your once cold stiff fingers pumping blood
in a luxuriousness that gathers to a lukewarm
rush now becoming spa-like disarming soup
where you are swimming with the glorious beasts
the polar bear whose whiteness is God and the
shimmering fishes who have been here before you
and can teach you a few things about swimming
and your mother and father and sisters and brothers
and the Christ-Sophia floating on her cross upholding others
and the Buddha with his empty begging bowl afloat
and the homeless exiles, and deadbeat strangers
and the corporate heads with their swirling logos
circling toward the miasmic centre of a vortex
and the goats and cows and dogs and wolves
lapping with you faithfully round and round the rim
their large panting tongues and solemn eyes—

and this goes on all day, all night, and on and all till
you all scald and drown or drowning wake together

Four Horsemen International

"Wake me up when the apocalypse comes"
my friend used to jest just before napping,
a kind of nodding tribute to William Blake
whose apocalypses were interior
wake up calls—dramaturgy of the soul

Enter more brutal imaginings
shelled out on foreign fields
by firms with names like
Four Horsemen International
offering lethal toy-like grenades

Ezekiel, Daniel, John of Patmos winced
at those horsemen Conquest, War, Famine, Death
gore rising to the horses' bridles,
yet we multiply horrors with our machines
that neither bleed nor cry

When the Saints Go Marching In

Let's have them galloping, skipping, bounding
let's have them rung in with tympani or sung with bel canto
or dancing like ladies or leaping lords

Let's have them chanting om or hallelujah
feasted or fasted, lumbering or still
or creeping in like fog on *little cat feet*

Rough golden codgers or slick newborns dropped
trailing clouds of gaiety, or glory
amazing themselves that there are so many ways to be

Let's have them ululating or rumbaing
shaking their glorious bodies
gleefully naked or clad in gold tissue

but please, please, don't let them be marching
marching, marching, goose-stepping and proud
as to jihad, crusade, or war

Let those feet ripple, trip, tinkle or caper

      peace

The Disarmed Heart

People arrive at a nuclear site
to dismantle rockets, bombs
and other weapons of mass destruction

Hands gently and tenderly
peel away pieces of a shield
from a large, viscous red heart

until a bit of the thundering organ
starts to show (just barely) beneath
the heavy apparatus

All you can see are hands of all sizes
and colours, moving over the encased drum
More and more of the fleshy heart

stirs underneath as the fingers
continue their work. At last
except for a few pieces of bronze

resembling armour plates, the heart
lies wholly exposed, thrumming
as the open palms fall away

Dwelling in Possibility

Cedars rise from duff
                their green names
        wide-open cadenzas

Concatenation of crows—
        nothing is as it is
              for long

When the Stones Rise

I speak not in hyperbole,
I speak in true words muted to their undertone,
choosing a pebble where you would a stone,
projecting pebbles to immensity.

—P.K. Page, from "The Understatement"

You thought about the nested worlds
but wanted more to see, hear, touch
to be, if only moment wise
earth music—since a single phrase
can make a maelstrom of the heart
empty the stony self into sea
or dust pool where the open eye
wry, enchanted, voids the void
gazing and gazing—clarity!
I speak—not in hyperbole

You speak in gardens
seeding blooms of sleep
where primrose disarranges time, the wild
musk rose's aromatic hush
stirs a geometry of hearts—
this earthly paradise, inverting cone
mountain, hut or vortex overturned
a sentence slides across bone
I speak in true words muted to their undertone

Something prefers the miniscule—pattern in broken
pattern, something whole lingering, who knows?
Adults look twice at an infant on the lawn
remembering things lost, things round
in the palm, when body knew most everything
something shaped to the hand, something on loan
You want no flying bolt or bomb
but vibrating signature of rock
earth token, living koan
choosing a pebble where you would a stone.

Now is all particular, particularized:
what the eye sees through you
and you through the eye, unknown
a laser sharpening, dissolved
These bright periwinkles under the window—
on their exact colour our words may not agree
Yet outside, rough bark of draughty Douglas fir
conceals a Persian miniature
secret calligraphy etched into bark
Distilling words, you open each sound free
projecting pebbles to immensity

The Possibilities of an Empty Page

*The spiritual dimensionality comes from the openness you must have to all
the possibilities of an empty page.*

—Don Domanski

Chestnut-backed chickadee
breaks from our backyard wildlife tree

whirls from her minute chamber
carved by last year's woodpeckers

(ingress-egress: barely a dervish blur
    quark of tail feathers)

Today, no resin, no residue of words responds:
no writing loops across the blank page

no sounding of dreamed notions
no spying of eggs, cream and rose

only the possibilities of an empty page—
    another kind of heaven

A Chant for the Opening of the Third Eye

If your eye is single, then your whole body shall be full of light.
—Matthew 6.22

Open the portal just above the eyes' yes
       where nothing is withheld

you who know
       this weary fluttering mind

Play on the double-fretted board of the forehead
       where two solid vertical bars embed themselves

Fill in the trenches where war's worries
       march their forced march through sand

Neither Botox, nor surgery, nor peels appeal
       but only old stirrings, fiery tinglings

just behind the centerpoint of the brow
       past the portal where angels post
       and nothing holds itself apart

Living Clothes

It's ordinary time. I'm roused by my alarm
      but not fully awake

The white door of the closet opens and
      behold! (Believe me, "behold" is the word)

a congregation of shimmering sheaths
      living garments flowing, singing

dancing, weaving, shining—kundalini earth fires
      yearning to move up the spine

become the body and extensions of the body
      transparent wings in chartreuse, magenta

rose, Prussian blue, orchid, lavender, sea-green
      fuchsia, blush, raw sienna, burnt orange, plum, and scarlet

Darling, I'm in the crayon box alive
      and all the colours have birthed distilled honey, wine

Goddess, I'm blushing
      This unified coronation dons the aquamarine swirling skirt

which falls over my head, twirls like a carousel
      and plunges into breath   this only ever now

Steady State Ekstasis

You follow Spirit up the ladder
or She follows you

Who's following whom?
you wonder, then land

on a rung of being
well past judgment

but not discernment
of the big landscape

to which you belong
with your thumping animal heart

and all its everyday amazements—
ant's trek, whale's bewildering song

Presto! As if this were enough
and so it is, as you finger

the wood's worn grain
imprints of bare feet

signs of others' playing
up and down the stair

for so it is, not ladder
but stair, spiralling

No thing above
no thing below—

only this intertwining
rest into action

this mystery
betwixt and between

from **Painter, Poet, Mountain:**
After Cézanne (2016)

We are a dazzling chaos. I stand before my motif, I lose myself in it.

One minute in the life of the world is going by. Paint it as it is!

—Paul Cézanne

Cézanne's Apples

Rounded sequences of sheen

        blush-green and russet

just where he left them   conversing

     corporeal

        counteracting planes

vanished vanishing points

       hundreds of brushstrokes

tang orange

     pang green

        wet colours self-adjusting

   to an entire tableau

holding tension of surface and field

     in the wholeness

        paints sometimes hold

I Close My Eyes

to hear

        the effortful

                effortless

breathing of his   blunt brush

not what is seen

        but the silences

before   in   after   within

        seeing

How His Colours

breathe azure

        think noir

                feel white-of-dusk

flash brushstrokes

        pool

           in the secrets

                of our abandoned

                    flesh

Hortense

The nineteen-year-old who posed
      for Cézanne in Paris
            still poses a few questions

Working-class model, bookbinder
      farmer's daughter, main squeeze
            then mother to Paul Jr.

To his friends, "La Boule"
      dumpling, yet she seems trim
            enough in his paintings
                  (affectionate sobriquet or jab?)

to Cezanne's father, his son's clandestine lover
      dubious, long unacknowledged
            unwelcome at the family estate
                then (after 17 years)   spouse

Anecdotes abound:
      she was profligate
            adored the casinos
      belittled his art
            lingered for an appointment with her seamstress
                at news of his death
                    bundled off his paintings for quick sale

Yet what of the hours when
        she sat immobile   silent
                as he ranged the enigma
                    of her upper lip
studied her apple faces
        just as he traced the clefts of his holy mountain
                through dashes and daubs of paint?

What remains of such intimate distances?
        A sleek chignon
                the sheen of a green-striped skirt
                    red armchair cupping
the folded hands

Quantum Mountain (*Étude* 1)

The more he tracked, traced
        circled, retraced her traces

the more she seemed to move
        away   almost to disappear

As he gaped   into her sun
        the limestone quarries fractured

her ochre morphed to a glimmering field
        web of trackless vibrating points, violet within of cells

The more she vanished
        the more she seemed to offer entrance

the more elusive her poetry
        the more it was utterly clear

and when he resigned completely
        the gaps opened

linearity, perspective
                failed

leaving only the mountain's mysterious signatures
                      places where the witnesses could gather

Mont Sainte-Victoire and Golden Ears

A stroll each day along the dike by the Fraser River
                 where eagles flap, flap, flap   and glide

to their posts in Douglas firs
                near peaks sacred to Coast Salish tribes

Compared to Victoire, the Golden Eyries are enormity
                Snow Queens   dazzling crowns

white beyond froth   beyond bone
                glaciated   cascades

If Cézanne could be airlifted here
                would he be undone?

I see his astounded eyes lower, close
                fling wide

Brush participates in spirals of light
                gaze leans into cliffs' breath

lifts to   falls from
                their icy gowns

He would paint himself into these goddesses
          as they are   who they are

                      who we are in them

Cézanne's *Baigneuses*

still bathing
        sky falling forever

into their bones
        (chartreuse grasses flowing

around and into
        relaxed limbs)

one leans into a tree
        that leans into her

some touching, others holding themselves   apart
        three here   five over there—

golden numbers
        everywhere   circulating

exactly how the world would look
        if earth were suddenly

                to compose our flesh

Digging His Blues

(a found poem)

Rilke dug the blues
in Van Gogh and the Impressionists
but Cézanne's blues knocked him out

Blues with "good conscience"
(blues with consciousness)

Blue turnings   tunings   burnings
summoned the poet
helped him find the words
that were always slipping

away:

"Egyptian shadow-blue
self-contained blue
listening blue
thunderstorm blue
bourgeois cotton blue
light cloudy bluishness
densely quilted blue
waxy blue ·
wet dark blue
juicy blue"

blue

Beware: Serious Tree Hugger

The olive tree was waiting for him.... He would touch it. He would talk to it. When he parted from it at night he would sometimes embrace it.... The wisdom of the tree entered his heart. "It's a living being," he said to me one day. 'I love it like an old friend. It knows everything about my life and gives me excellent advice. I should like to be buried at its feet.'

—Henri Gasquet

They all painted olive trees
                        Matisse, Monet
Van Gogh   a whole grove of them outside Arles
twisting now as it did when Vincent first came
to the sanatorium

But of Cézanne alone was it said
he spoke to his olive
touched and embraced her
savouring her salt
in thick *beurres blancs*
over chicken or duck

I thought of him at the *marchés* in Aix
when I brought home bagfuls
of the small, black ones

like those perhaps from the olive
at his studio at Les Lavres

for he bought the land
precisely because of the tree

Despite C's request
he was not buried under the olive
but buries and raises himself daily
                              in his olive tree paintings

"He had no real friends except trees"
                    said his friend Henri

The Power of Vegetables

"With an apple
I will
astonish
Paris"
said Paul Cézanne

though it wasn't just the apple
but the many seeings
one perspective from the right
another from the left

another from above
another from below
and so on
all in one apple

cross-dimensionality of appleness
in an ordinary apple
one might use for pies
or apple sauce

"The day is
coming
when a single
carrot

freshly observed
will set off
a revolution"
he quipped

I'm still revolving in my dreams
         the matter of the carrot

The Gardener Vallier Speaks

Under the lime tree in the garden
he painted me for the last time

a few days after they brought him home
when he fell on the road in a storm

So many hours I had posed for him
not minding the passage of time

the long breaks from work
occasions to sit quietly remembering this and that

We talked some
but mostly we worked in silence

and I remember
how I bought him herbs

massaged his limbs
when he wouldn't let anyone else touch him

I, the only one there when he died

Some say he painted himself
into me and I into him

our beards and peasant hats
the dark background against a white shirt

crossed legs

           the gentle flow of hands

Such a Proceeding

Out of emergency

      the poems & paintings emerge

         simply there

            whistling

     from songbird's beak

        blue

          transparent

                       gone

New Poems

from Lineage

The Valley Spirit never dies.
It is called the Mysterious Female.
And the doorway of the Mysterious Female
is the base from which Heaven and Earth spring.
It is there within us all the time.
Drink from it you who will;
it never runs dry.

—Lao Tzu, from *Tao Te Ching*

from Negative Capability:
A Suite for John Keats

4

I am certain of nothing but of the holiness of the Heart's affections and the
truth of Imagination—What the imagination seizes as Beauty must be
truth—whether it existed before or not—for I have the same Idea of all
our Passions as of Love: they are all in their sublime, creative of essential
Beauty.

(Keats to Benjamin Bailey, November 22, 1817)

In the land of uncertainties
You are certain
Of the great nothings
That are therefore
Somethings, like
Beauty and Truth—
Those showings
That are not abstract

Especially when held in a
Spider's rainbow web or
The slenderness of the spider
Herself who slips in
From the cold
Flirting her silk
By the window—the one
You lifted to safety

Or when a Northern Flicker
Slow-times time with its red cap
And spotted vest
Hovering near the fir,
Up and gone:

Such vestiges,
Footprints on air
We stand on tip toe to hear.

8

[N]othing startles me beyond the Moment. The setting Sun will always set
me to rights—or if a Sparrow come before my Window I take part in its
existence and pick about the Gravel.
(to Benjamin Bailey, November 22, 1817)

What easeful slipping into pulse, nerves, heart
Of sparrow, robin, wren, or chickadee,
Piquant hummingbird's blurred wings,
Crow's scuffing up of dust under the ledge.

Tail feathers flick within your mystery eye,
Your cocked head turns again, still listening
To music of a breath held in a beak.
Bird Muse, I feel you ever near and far

Then join you, pecking, where the low sun falls.

9

"Negative Capability, that is when [we are] capable of being in uncertainties, Mysteries, doubts, without any irritable reaching after fact & reason...."
(to George and Tom Keats, Dec. 21-27, 1817)

Incapably capable here in mist,
Doubting all but being in the world

Without any petty, fractious
Reaching, grasping

After fact, the verifiable—no
Folding into factoids.

So we become the all
And nothing of stardust

Yearning backwards
Into presence.

14

The innumerable compositions and decompositions which take place between the intellect and its thousand materials before it arrives at that trembling delicate and Snail-horn perception of beauty....
(To B.R. Haydon, April 8, 1818)

My garden spade uncovered a golden snail
With its Fibonacci spiral shell of armour,
Its delicate horn waving in the morning air

And I thought of you composing your "Ode to Psyche"
Just at the moment when the lovers' lips
No longer touched but had not said goodbye.

Cupid and Psyche, not discomposed,
But recomposed as in a living still life,
He but part a god, she not yet a goddess

While the delicate snail made its way down
Into the un-striving sod, an intellect
Shaped by and shaping its materials

In the composing, decomposing world,
Perceived and so made new.

15

I compare human life to a large Mansion of Many Apartments ... the in-
fant or thoughtless Chamber ..., the Chamber of Maiden-Thought ..., and
the dark passages. We are in a Mist....

(To J.H. Reynolds, May 3, 1818)

I am walking through a brick house with scratched floors,
Dolls aligned on the bed, red shorts and halter top laid out,

Touching the books, fairy tales, *Journeys through Bookland.*
I am pre-thought, thoughtful-less, I am play, thinking I can walk

Forever, a figure on an urn caught in breath and eye,
My eyes grope the walls, then I am suddenly a teen,

Such a trooper, pushing my way past doors to another
Spaciousness, where the rooms vibrate. I know I want

To be a poet, I want to be a teacher, I falter and fall,
Rise and step into a larger room, touch the graffiti on the walls,

Stroke the layers, keep groping, moving past doors
Into responsibilities, my child at play, the daily work,

Retiring shadows, and now the Keats room, the
Not nothing room, the darkening room of passages

Pass my visual field. I am in a mist, unknowing,
Where death, even-handed death, is sleeping

And everything is a Mystery, and we, Keats
And I and you and me and Keats are not alone.

21

Call the world if you Please "The vale of Soul-making."
(To George and Georgiana Keats, April 21, 1819)

No systematic theologian,
yet you parsed the mysteries

With questions like Job
Wailed from the dung heap.

Why pain, why sorrow, why loss?
You didn't seek a salvation scheme

Of punishment, redemption,
By a God outside the world,

But told a story of how we forge
Our very souls, distinct Identities.

Like the mystics, you spoke of us
As sparks, atoms of perfection,

Of how we are God.
For the sparks are pure,

Bliss-bathed; yet we must go to school
To make them shine.

In your story, Intelligence,
Heart, and the world of elemental space

Act on each other to burnish
Sparks, an active process working

Through weal and woe,
Till the busy mind lowers

Itself into the heart and flourishes.
For the heart is always core.

22

I will call the World a School, and I will call the human heart the
Hornbook used in that School, and I will call the Child about to read the
Soul made from that school and its Hornbook.
(To George and Georgiana Keats, April 21, 1819)

In elementary school I had a pen, ring binder,
And lift-lid desk. Certainly no hornbook,

No paddle-shaped board of wood, covered
On both sides with pictures, alphabets, sayings:

"A dog will bite a thief at night."
"Thy life to mend this book attend."

Yet still, we enter the school of the world
Through a curriculum of bruises,

Begin reading the braille of our hearts,
Blood flow, word flow, pulsing within,

Becoming souls, co-creating what we are:
Living books made from animal skins or trees.

Curious sounds rise and fall with the breath.
Promptings of water, air, earth, fire

Transform admonitions into wisdom
As we ingest, enflesh the curious letters.

26

I have an habitual feeling of my real life having passed, and that I am lead-ing a posthumous existence…. I can scarcely bid you good-bye, even in a letter. I always made an awkward bow.

(To Charles Brown, Nov. 30, 1820)

I'm leading a posthumous existence
Somewhere between the coils of earth and sky,
England's green cradle now at a distance,
Since bustling Rome is where I've come to die.
My pen and living hand have dug a site,
Foundation, cavern, what you choose to know
Of words that fall with bodies into night—
Unknowing, where our wasted shadows go.
Worlds end for humans, species cruel and kind,
Who still destroy the base by which they live.
Yet breath that circulates in body-mind,
Earth-fettered, earth-released, helps us forgive
And sing farewells and greetings to the now.
Through love *I always made an awkward bow.*

Who Am I?

Conscientious and impulsive
        child singing arias in an apple tree

transparent apples gathered in my lap
        russet and green. I am

bough-born
        cosmos-thrown

constricted and flourishing
        throned in a seat of crossed limbs

startled, looking around
        curious fearful bold

singing arias to unseen hosts
        from inside a tree

Language Alive

The language
winks back
running its hands through our hair

through old Magnolia's
thick creamy
petals

swollen leaves
brown-edged
drift into the earth

Dear Emily

Your miniature cabinets
cosmic as Walt's barbaric yawps
yield new antiquities
star-flung vaults

spare and grand
in a sparrow's
metric pecking
to a hermit beat

white nun—all and zero sum
quiet
not mum

Peonies

spring-
load the air

near tremors
of ruby-throated

humming-
bird

chestnut-backed
chick-

a-dee
dee-dee

The Archeology of Writing

Evolving fingers
clasped pens (plumes)

Cursive script rushed onto snowy pages

Dexterous hands now peck
(letters as music—music as letters)

on screens lofted to cyberspace

Alternate cloud of unknowing
mulls our transmissions

alphabets tango
word tangles, world-tangled

meaning hums
drafts   (light drifting to light)

sift through
liminal spaces

Something
simple as a line is

singing us home
the poems still writing us down

Grace

Right now, let's say
as we are gagging
on our most
unruminated words
regretting our regrets
self-recriminating
our self-recriminations

let's say for an instant
a sword slashes
all that self-criticism
draws back a veil
to just this:
wisdom face
Sophia, Compassion

not forgiving
since there is
nothing to forgive
but seeing us
as we are—
infinitely
worthy

Venturing Into Closets

In dad's closet   neckties sag
in dissolute career

red, white, and blue   martial flags
creased   wine-dipped

sagging bomber jacket
           smelling of leather and old time

His slightness and height
          before the drag of late middle age

where I stalled:
        remembering ties

Dying   he signed off
          "Have a good life"
as if pointing
to some heavenly midway

where once his living hand
           traced Ursa Major

beyond the flakes of "I"

Lao Tzu Meets the Progress Trap

A tree as great as a human's embrace springs from a small shoot.

—Lao Tzu

Capitalism is not sentience
like these breathing trees

Who are you, Lao Tzu?
Sage fresh-born from the Tao

Our neighbour's acreage is
filled with western red cedars

hemlocks, Douglas firs
rooted like you, and nameless

(though we give them names)
purifiers of the shared air

Yet for our neighbour only obstacles
so he summons hackers, hewers

excavators, diggers, screaming
chainsaws. Elders thud

Banshee wind moans
among falling limbs

Full of purpose his truck
scuttles up and down the drive

Are there city covenants?
Some, but seldom enforced

When a woman phones the township
to challenge his doings

he pulls out his mantra: "A man can do
what he wants to do on his own private land"

One day Lao Tzu climbs his drive
to survey the wreckage

stoops to touch ravaged limbs
Is old Lao Tzu trespassing?

"Great harm," he sighs
Owner drives by

Owner cannot hear
Lao Tzu's ancient voice

A woman weeps
Lao Tzu whispers in her ear:

Nothing abides outside the Tao
flowing around and through

breaking down stone

"The Tao continues," she interjects,
"but what of us caught

in the progress trap
manipulated by corporate kings?

Greed-ravaged Gaia
the only home we know

In time's breath, surely
there must be some effective resistance.

Lao Tzu, how does your wisdom flow
into the arms of a more active yielding?

How do we stand with the trees?
Who will awaken

the Mysterious Female
who plays in all things

and is at the base of all things
the base from which heaven and earth spring?"

Mother Sea

You sailed into our bones before we were born
Nothing is as we know it without you

We are your body, your microbes,
skin boats—

ocean lovers and betrayers

We are particles your currents made live
but we hardened and became particulates

We are plastic prodigals
Our selves won't break down

Though you regenerate over eons
we may not unless we turn, soften

recycle, weep
We are bailing, we are refugees

We are dying
We are afraid

You have made
these motley coracles we are

though we think ourselves
floating on the surface

We go deep
we go down

with you, or turn, turn
repent with the prophets

into our change

Strait of Juan de Fuca / Stone Flow
(1973 & 2016)

At twenty-six, a rose-coloured
      milky quartz stone   rises singular to my eye

I pluck it from its bed of sand
      rinse its rust-streaked sides

feel its warming, tide-polished
      light roll between forefinger and thumb

drop it pocket-deep, carry it home
      set it on my writing desk near the typewriter—

sacred relic from Mother Sea

Why did I keep the gift for decades
      then discard it in the garden during a move?

(I see it kelp-wrapped, wet, a singing sheen)

My skin has become a moving parchment
      sometimes swept clean

Ocean gifts gathered, abandoned,
      more prized than gems

healing stones: odes to time
   round, unrenowned, oblong

beings   still flourishing
      in circles wet with spray

Dear Sophia

I surrender
to all

you are
gathering

blue-green
shards

energy-
light

one body
bowing

not as to a king
but to what flows

what we embody
further in—

       the Thou
of now

Mycorrhizal Fungi

Fingers touch down on
imagined neural networks

underground root systems
where fungi decompose nutrients

Firs and cedars draw them up
to build wood fibre

transform CO_2 to oxygen:
        ancient miracle

clean air, reduced carbon
deep breathing   from deep time

Darwinian secret:
        evolutionary co-operation

motherliness stretching
        waving boughs

through heart-worn legacies
        skyward

Firs, cedars
        (sentinel nurses)

still day-ing,
        night-ing

        their continuous genealogies

A Mottled Leaf

Walking the labyrinth
of pacing time
time thrusts eyeward
one seared leaf

Five yellowish bands
browning
age spots
on darkening hands

Some primal
wet greenness remains
where I too am being absorbed
into everything

Roots Dancing

You could say roots
        squidged as they are
between dark heaps of soil
        shivering and soaked
don't dance
           but you'd be wrong

for in that dry, wet
          wondering dark
they curiously minuet
           drawing near   and apart
wiggle-stepping   spreading
           corkscrewing   around stones
weaving lateral-vertical designs
        criss-crossing
               turning
delving, snaking
                      spiralling wide
clasping and unclasping
hands
           in the dark ground

Roots are chords

                    (cords)   fluent thrummings

drawing water

                 from dance's core

while trees

                 their lanky siblings
                       thrust themselves skyward

Yes, you'd be wrong

                 about roots
                     not dancing
                           and soaked
simply sitting shivering   between dark clods of soil

hunching together

                 immobile

Ice Neurons on Young Lake

(Cariboo region of British Columbia)

My husband and I deer-step
onto the frozen surface of Young Lake
mostly safe, though some patches leer

Soon we are gliding, walking on water
pausing to be gathered in by silence
Further down, designs, curious formations:

"Something like amorphous amoebas" he says
"But with dancing tentacles," I venture
"Ice spiders," he suggests

More and more, each singular
as a snowflake, crystals
begun from fractures

sheens with dark centres
glimmer in the sudden sun:
"Not exactly spiders

more like neurons,"
I muse.
"I've seen them in photos

cells with arms
resembling nerve synapses
Ice synapses."

Home, I Google brain neurons:
nerve cells clasping hands in the dark
Indra's net hidden in the world's body

whole galaxies similarly shaped
ice art, brain cells, universe—
one

A Wedding Villanelle for Ingrid and Doug

Set me as a seal upon your heart …
for love is as strong as death.

—"The Song of Songs"

Set me as a seal upon your heart
impressed like golden light in marigold's
or daisy's flush where *love is strong as death*

Her nimble otter-mind slips into streams
his black bear-spirit joins in the play
They press their seals on complementary hearts

Their kindness kindles kindness in each other
this constancy returning keeps them whole
Reciprocal dreamers find love strong as death

The Holy brims in deep equality
where listening listens as they share their days
with signatures inscribed upon the heart

He ventures into novel ways to see;
helping others be heard becomes her way
Their children, rooted, know love outlasts death

Slow steady love for planetary health
creative tendrils flourish, life sustained
where hope has set a seal upon our hearts
and death and love in process raise one flame

The Names

...when we touch these sacred but exhausted
Names, these wounded scattered petals
Which have come out of the oceans of love and fear
Something still remains, a sip of water...
                    —Pablo Neruda, from "Gautama Christ"

When we thrust or hurl
these bounded names
mysterious as dark matter
when we seize these sacred but exhausted

signs, symbols, signatures
moon-pointers,
smart bombs may smartly strike, but sometimes
names, these wounded scattered petals

find soul soil
manifest mystery
break from a point of nothingness
out of oceans of love and fear

then we cup them in our hands
turn them over like seashells
listen to their layered soundings where
something still remains   a sip of water

Footbaths for Learners

We are all learners, with feet needing most
to touch earth, feel the dust from which we came
and which we are shining

How feet long to sink into moss
grip down, be soothed, smoothed
washed and kissed

our Achilles tendons wept over, caressed
arches cupped till nerves sign
love, sparks rise from toes

When someone bends to another
the recipient may turn, reciprocate
I washing your feet, you washing mine

Post-operative feet become operatic
sing home, smile with the animals:
dog's pads, cat's digits

Old feet share kicks of infants
assert their bright I Am's
into the vibrating air

Yet feet are most free
when bonded to forest floors
or bright lengths of sand

How they arch, stretch, dance
our beautiful listening feet
carrying us across

the seas of time and space

Mandala

Lao Tzu dances
        yin-yang

Confucius points above
        and below

Moses cracks open
        the chestnuts of cosmic law

Buddha is a lotus
        cupped in a bowl

Mohammed surrenders
        what is surrendering him

Socrates turns
        on his female Muse's tripod

Jesus, two-winged
        rises dying, dies rising

Mary Magdalene
        uncensored, dispenses myrrh

Rabi'a dances silk
        through Rama's hair

White Rose of Heaven
       rhapsodizes bliss

all from a single point
             of nothingness

Elegiac: George Whipple
(May 24, 1927-May 29, 2014)

No glibness for my friend the poet
who spoke straight with wry curves
airy basilicas grounding into earth-studies

I spread out his books on the kitchen counter
counting the ways he spoke
leaf through his whimsical sketches

then the reams of postcards
letters tumbling, Thanksgiving, Easter
Christmas, "just for nothing" cards

one imaging a sky-full of cumulus—
nothing besides

Clipped-out cartoons: man sitting
in armchair, calling to his wife
"I'm in here, rereading the great poets, myself among them"

(For him, a cautionary tale about pride—
in his case, indubitably true)

A letter: "Thank you very much
for your kind and generous
response to *The Seven Wonders of the Leg*
                    Such feedback is precious and so rare"

Speaking of "wonders of the leg"
my eye rests now on his gift
that one day arrived in a box:

ceramic carousel Pegasus
twirling on a musical stand, neck decked
with soft clusters of pale pink roses

violet wings aloft, right foot broken—
            a wounded Pegasus
What can words do but sigh

sing May, the month he signed off?:
            I came but never arrived; I go but do not depart

A Magnolia Chalice for Glenda

(d. April 17, 2011)

Magnolia presence at full flower
lifts into setting sun

as Glenda into mystery
who so many days

(carrying her terror of cancer)

danced with sun and moon
together in one sky

an opening cup
graced by shot silk pink

Power Dream

My father thought the world
of me, thought everything

was possible, thought worlds into me
believed I was a new world

"You did a fine job," he said.
"I could never do what you do with language"

But it's what language does with me
when
shhh   ah

the ground again rises
a green, cushioning field

the one that took him away
where he reaches me still

(stilled)
          by his living voice

Faith

(based on Odilon Redon's charcoal drawings, *My Noirs*)

has grown hope-hearted
during her sleep
those steep *noirs*

where numb-footed nightmares
toss off their boots
lift into dawn

Who would have guessed
distress could bring
such commodious wings?

Feelers and Eyes That Know You

We have long been watching you
                 with long millennial looks
you who so curiously probe
               our earth
                        with your strange desires
not only to know but   to control
               waterways, fireways, airways

We have fled and hidden
               from your cruelties, obsessions
obscene massacres—
our huntings and gatherings
               no match for your consumption

You have peeled away layer after layer of the earth
               driving always for more—
though you are smaller than our grizzlies
               less lithe than our snow leopards

Your songs are mostly crude yawps
               compared to arias of the thrush—
your jet planes less graced
               than hawk's glide

We grieve your combative blights and despoilings
         proud self-woundings   mass-mutilations

Our wolves contemplate sunsets
Our ruminants too ponder their deaths
yet we do not boast in our
         diverse languages
         too subtle for your ears, saying:
                  "I alone Am and know I Am"

Yet despite your ravagings
         we sense an enormous tenderness
         the sometimes softness of your voices and hands
when we lean together at the fire
         common creatures of a common home

Convivium

(38th Anniversary)

Living
together

one
symbiosis

moon
feast

bounded
in boundless

love
song

Two seasoned horses
chanting

each for each

remembering
how

at the cabin
in spring they

filly and colt
first grazed

gazed
together

at the cantering
moon

Adrift, Seeking and Waiting

(for Joy)

What better place
to be than in this boat

the common one
everyday hull

of blessed nothings?

Cosmic consciousness
Enlightenment

mostly only words

Yet we are in it
with the illusion

of stepping
out or in

Doing nothing
we deepen

adrift
seeking and waiting

Poem for the Spring Solstice

Be generous with your praise
The rainbow doesn't stint
Say a brave hello to troubles

Walk your tearful yes
into swept cedars
whose crowns have been broken
by a fierce wind

Nothing divine charges a fee
Everything is charged with love

Appendix: Selections from Early Chapbooks

Poetry, Painting & Music are the three Powers in [Humans] of Conversing with Paradise.

—William Blake, "A Vision of the Last Judgment"

Gnosis

1

Firstverb grows ears
In the vast drum
Stretched taut across
Earth's womb:

A hearing

2

Lightning bolts
To the four corners
Whirling down the channels
Of the wind:

A speaking

3

Firstverb finds eyes
In the deep sun
Charioted slowly under
Earth's crust:

A seeing

4

Lightstream leaps
From the twelve gates
Singing in the pearls
Of awareness:

A knowing

Will the Transformation

(after Rilke)

Will the transformation that you cannot will
But willingly aspire to will entire.
Will the restitution heart cannot restore
But leave your mode of thinking and desire.

And willingly the condition will will you
Unto a wider, more expansive view.
Refuse delight in any binding toy—
The nets and trammels to your central joy.

Photosynthesis

(for Mark)

I have loved before
But not these winds
Breaking my heart.

I have loved
But not this narrow house
Split wide by breathing hold.

Prophetic cedar
Atmosphere of fir
An ordering of pines.

These things I cannot separate
From you—the fragrant grove
Against the sky's intense reserve.

Not plants alone, but
Everything eats light.
Sun alchemized in lacery
Of grass, leaf, flower.

This photosynthesis
That we and angels make
Forms in the heart
A mountain slowly green.

Have you loved and been released
Swift, without recall
To drink these worlds—

Spring turning to display
Her deepening golds
The hallowing of life
In winey roses overflow?

As Love Is a Transforming Power

In the brimming dark
We laid ourselves down
You beside me—
Male with female.

By the sounding lake
The black bears walked
One by one their
Shaggy walk.

A slender vision
Grappled in your brain.
What centre of the golden
Asphodel?

These temporal powers held.
A spiritual rest reclaimed
Our bodies bound and wound
In mutual surrender

Of you and me
Beneath the windy tree
Within the clasp
Of images and words.

Locus

At the very centre of the world
An emerald pool stands
In a heron stillness.

The pool's green
Is not a colour
But a space
Whose revelation
Is itself.

At the very centre of the world
An emerald pool stands
In a heron stillness.

The Vision of Denis Maximian (excerpt)

There is heaven all the way to Heaven,
For he said, "I am the Way."

—Catherine of Siena

And if I speak as one drawn
From city to city
And talk of heavenly things,
Fire-tipped fruit
Unimaginable trees
Recognize not me
But the place
Recognize the gifts
Not me
Keep me from being to myself
Enough.

Not me
But what we are to be
Thou and I

Feathers

I was old and sleepy
when the scales fell from my eyes.
Then I heard a sound of feathers from out there
Coming to make nests in my sight.

The time? I kept it
sorting them all
According to hue.

Green-white, rose-gold
Purple-brown, silver-white,
They fell from my hands
Into four piles
Magically, like the seasons,
And turned at night
Into women whose soft wings
Whirled me in a storm
Of eyelids closing.

From wondercircles of sleep
I touched an entire farm of beasts,
Silver, gold-fleeced
Moving up and down the ladder of my breath.

Shining tears ran down their eyes
Washing away the tints of barn and sky,
Till all colours were but
The presence of vast wings
Against the equinoxes of the dream.

More than this I do not remember
But that I was old and sleepy.
Yet I have dreamed beyond death
And now wait ever by the door
With clear, pure eyes
Wearing only this cloak
of numberless feathers—

Knowing that it too must fall away.

Villanelle

A city raised by sound within the heart
Untouched, unfathomed by the light of day
A circle spreading where all circles start

Whose radius extends beyond the chart
Cartographers retrace who lose the way
To cities raised by sound within the heart.

Taut bows release the Heraclitean dart
Uniting with the target of their play:
A circle spreading where all circles start.

For every spark and speech there is a part
Within each one to mirror and relay
The city raised by sound within the heart.

So now in utter blankness let us start
To hold between us what the angels pray—
A circle spreading where all circles start.

That we may shape the meaning of our art
Enfold within our being as we may
A city raised by sound within the heart
A circle spreading where all circles start.

Tree

Pierce, pierce my roots to heaven
Crown me with choiring birds.
Thorn my brow with arcs of fire.
Feed me star-food,
That from this dark and inauspicious shell
My heavy boughs may wake with dancing flowers.

Metaphysics

Within your eyes a pool awakes;
A pure and glancing mind partakes
The moving footfall of the stars,
The crystal circles holding far
Beyond the moon's astonishment
And all the warm world's ravishment.

Beyond the turning worlds of sense
I see within your face the hints
Of something larger that coheres,
That maps the greater hemispheres,
A word, a spark, a fractured gleam
Of God's incarnate central dream.

Though forest citadels of rhyme
Collapse against the pulse of time,
You're in the One who is in you:
This is the secret Jesus knew
Who caught you in his fiery hold
And made you human, lasting gold.

A Dream of William Blake

He was working at a Lazarus on an easel
When I broke the bright circle of his thought,
I a student with a few pressing questions
About Jerusalem, the fourfold bride.

He who had been dead or asleep
And was now alive forevermore
Stood a little to one side as if
Listening with his whole imagination.

From the easel or behind I heard
The sound of cerements breaking,
Swaddling clothes falling from new flesh.
At that moment he and Lazarus were one.

Before I could be sure, he read me,
Knew me for a seeker out of Ulro,
A pilgrim bound for Golgonooza
With a pack of books strapped to my back.

"Sure, my old stuff is fine in its way,"
He said with a sloughing of skin,
Then pointed with flashing hand
To eternity where his new works evolve.

Trillium and Unicorn

White trillium enlarges
into its day, trifoliate,
triptych among plants.

Soft-maned unicorn
of studious blue eyes
nuzzles its figured leaves.

In the aromatic dark
of a spice garden,
make the fiction real

so real it serves the sense
and lives as large as everything
that stoops to be imagined.

Acknowledgements

Thanks to Inanna Publications for undertaking the publication of *Into the Open: Poems New and Selected*, a volume that is both a retrospective and synthesis of my work over four decades. Publisher Luciana Ricciutelli and publicist Renée Knapp are indefatigable in their honouring of the divine and human feminine in her many modes.

Katerina Fretwell, my intuitive and diligent editor, has kindly brought a visual artist's eye, a poet's mind and heart, and a musician's ear to this collaborative work—a venture requiring much time, energy, and commitment.

Deep thanks to Russell Thornton, whose insightful Introduction gave me back my poems, helping me see newness in both their emergence and development. Without his penetrating eye, I would not have realized how the magnolia had secretly bloomed into a central metaphor in my work, appearing, disappearing, and reappearing in surprising places.

I would like to acknowledge the publishers of the following volumes of my poetry: *Conversing with Paradise* (Golden Eagle Press, 1986); *Locutions* (Ekstasis Editions, 1995); *Light Housekeeping* (Ekstasis Editions, 1997); *Veil/ Unveil* (The St. Thomas Poetry Series, 1997); *Into the Open* (Golden Eagle Press, 1999); *The Altering Eye* (Borealis Press, 2000); *Flying Wounded* (University Press of Florida, 2000); *Common Longing* (Mellen Poetry Press, 2001); *At the Mercy Seat* (Ronsdale Press, 2003); *A Plot of Light* (Oolichan Books, 2004); *Lifting the Stone* (Seraphim Editions, 2007); *Demeter Goes Skydiving* (University of Alberta Press, 2011); *The*

Disarmed Heart (The St. Thomas Poetry Series, 2014); *Painter, Poet, Mountain: After Cézanne* (Quattro Books, 2016).

I also wish to thank my husband Mark Haddock, who helped me self-publish the early chapbooks: *Motions of the Hearts* (1978), *Kindling* (1979), and the full-length volume *Into the Open* (Golden Eagle Press, 1999) in its first incarnation. My previous publishers and editors include: Frank Tierney (Borealis Press), Richard Olafson (Ekstasis Editions), David Kent (The St. Thomas Poetry Series), Ron Hatch (Ronsdale Press), Ron Smith (Oolichan Books), Maureen Whyte (Seraphim Editions), Peter Midgley (The University of Alberta Press), and Allan Briesmaster (Quattro Books). Thanks to Ted Staunton (The Iona Press), Mona Fertig (Mother Tongue Press), Rhonda Batchelor (Reference West), and David Zieroth (The Alfred Gustav Press) for first publishing suites from these volumes as chapbooks.

Some of the poems from my unpublished volume *Lineage* have appeared in the following:
"Venturing Into Closets," in *Contemporary Verse 2* (Summer 37:1), 2014.
"Elegiac (George Whipple, May 24, 1927-May 29, 2014)," in *The Dalhousie Review*, 94:2 (Summer 2014), 287.
"A Mottled Leaf," and "Ice Neurons on the Surface of Young Lake," in *Sage-ing with Creative Spirit, Grace and Gratitude*. Ed. Karen Close. Kelowna, British Columbia: The Okanagan Institute (No. 15, Spring 2015), 5-9.
"Feelers and Eyes That Know You," and "Roots Dancing," in *Cascadia Review* (Summer 2015).
"Grace," in *Dialogue: Canada's Independent Voices Magazine*. Ed. Maurice J. King & Janet Hicks King. (Vol. 28, No. 3; Nanaimo, BC, April 2015).
"Lao Tzu Meets the Progress Trap," in *Canadian Woman Studies/les cahiers de la femme*, Vol. 31, No. 1, 2016.

The poem "Mother Sea" was inspired by visual artist Erica Grimm, who requested I write a poem on oceans for her workshop, Rising Tides and Skin Boats, an eco-art socially engaged workshop that was part of Surrey, BC's Environmental Extravaganza, May 17, 2017.

"Mandala" will be published in *Presence: An International Journal of Spiritual Direction*, March 2018.

I hold in heart and mind those who have encouraged me over the years and provided helpful feedback during the selection process: Mark Haddock, E.D. Blodgett, J.S. Porter, James Clarke, Antoinette Voûte Roeder, and Lee Johnson.

I would like to thank The Memoiristas, my creative non-fiction writing group (Kate Braid, Heidi Greco, Joy Kogawa, Elsie K. Neufeld, and Marlene Schiwy) for their support. Gratitude also is due to my former poetry reading group, The Compossibles: Kate Braid, Pam Galloway, Ellen McGinn, Susan MacRae, Dawn Petten, Tana Runyan, Sandy Shreve, Leslie Timmins, and Bibiana Tomasic. Thanks to my daughter Claire Haddock for her faithful love and support, and to fellow poet, spoken word artist, playwright, activist, and friend, Penn Kemp.

Finally, I would like to acknowledge some deceased poets who have inspired me. My first poetry mentor Robin Blaser called such luminaries the "Great Companions"—those who have entered what Blake calls "Eternity": the anonymous author of the Homeric Hymn to Demeter, Dante Alighieri, S. T. Coleridge, John Keats, Emily Dickinson, Gwendolyn MacEwan, Denise Levertov, Margaret Avison, P.K. Page, and George Whipple.

Photo: Mark Haddock

Susan McCaslin's *Into the Open: Poems New and Selected* represents a synthesis of poems drawn from four decades of her calling to the rigors and delights of poetry. Susan has published fourteen volumes of poetry and nine chapbooks. Recently, she published a memoir about the contemplative life, *Into the Mystic: My Years with Olga* (Inanna, 2014). Her previous volume of poetry, *Painter, Poet, Mountain: After Cézanne* (2016) engages with the life and works of the Post-Impressionist painter Paul Cézanne. Her early *Letters to William Blake* (1997) was heralded by poet P.K. Page, and a more recent volume, *Demeter Goes Skydiving* (2012), was shortlisted for the Dorothy Livesay BC Book Prize for Poetry and was the first-place winner of the Alberta Book Publishing Award (Robert Kroetsch Poetry Book Award) in 2012. She lives in Fort Langley, British Columbia, where she initiated the Han Shan Poetry Project to help save an endangered rainforest near her home.

Editor: Katerina Vaughan Fretwell's eighth poetry book, which includes her art, *Dancing on a Pin*, was published by Inanna in 2015. Five of the poems placed as Runner Up in *subTerrain's* Outsider poetry contest, 2015, and *Dancing on a Pin* won Fretwell a spot in the International Festival of Author's annual Battle of the Bards at Harbourfront, 2016. Her seventh book, *Class Acts*, also published by Inanna, 2013, was included in Kerry Clare's Most Important Books of 2013: Poetry in the online 49th Shelf. One of the poems, a sestina called "Kissing Cousins," was a finalist in *Descant* magazine's Winston Collins Poetry Prize, 2013. Two of her cat poems from the manuscript *Kat's Eye and Celtic Knots* appeared in Canadian Authors Association Niagara Region's anthology *The Bannister*. Short Shrift and Swat Shot Sestina, from the manuscript *We Are Malala,* will appear in *The Windsor Review* online. Fretwell's poetry and art reside across Canada and in Denmark, Japan, the United States and Wales. She won First Prize Watercolour in Toronto at Artfocus Group Show, 2001. Her poetic sequence *Quartzite Dialogues* was set to music by Michael Horwood and performed thrice at the Festival of the Sound in 1999 and 2014 and once in Japan,1999, at the Takefu Music Centre.

Introduction: Russell Thornton's *The Hundred Lives* was shortlisted for the 2015 Griffin Poetry Prize. His *Birds, Metals, Stones & Rain* was shortlisted for the 2013 Governor General's Award for Poetry, the Raymond Souster Award and the Dorothy Livesay B.C. Book Prize. His other titles include *The Human Shore, House Built of Rain, A Tunisian Notebook*, and *The Fifth Window*. His poems have been included in anthologies such as *The Best Canadian Poetry in English 2012* and *Open Wide a Wilderness: Canadian Nature Poems* and have appeared in translation in Greek, Romanian, and Ukrainian. He lives in North Vancouver, B.C.